Why Torture Is Wrong,
and the People Who Love Them
and Other Political Plays

Christopher Durang works published by Grove Press:

The Marriage of Bette and Boo

Laughing Wild and *Baby with the Bathwater*

Christopher Durang Explains It All for You
(volume includes:
The Nature and Purpose of the Universe
'dentity Crisis
Titanic
The Actor's Nightmare
Sister Mary Ignatius Explains It All for You
Beyond Therapy)

Betty's Summer Vacation

Miss Witherspoon and *Mrs. Bob Cratchit's Wild Christmas Binge*

Why Torture Is Wrong, and the People Who Love Them and Other Political Plays

CHRISTOPHER DURANG

Grove Press
New York

Published simultaneously in Canada
Printed in the United States of America

FIRST EDITION

ISBN: 978-0-8021-4567-3

Grove Press
an imprint of Grove/Atlantic, Inc.
841 Broadway
New York, NY 10003

Distributed by Publishers Group West

www.groveatlantic.com

12 13 14 15 16 17   10 9 8 7 6 5 4 3 2 1

Contents

Introduction

Growing up, I was oblivious to politics. I was interested in theater and plays and musicals, and also old movies. And my parents and the extended family of aunts, uncles, and grandparents also seemed not too focused on politics.

But twice in my life I got jolted into a strong focus on what was happening in our country. The first was the Vietnam War when I was a teenager. And the second was when my critically acclaimed play *Sister Mary Ignatius Explains It All for You* was attacked by conservative religious groups who found the play offensive and wanted it shut down.

I grew up in a Catholic family. The two options in life were to get married and have children, or to become a priest or nun. We went to Mass every Sunday morning. If you didn't go to Mass, you committed a mortal sin; and a mortal sin sent you to hell. (You could skip Mass if you were sick, though, or if there was a nuclear attack.) After Mass we and many other churchgoers stopped and got doughnuts and crumb cakes. They were delicious.

When I wasn't thinking about writing plays or being an actor (which interested me from age eight on), I did wonder if I should become a priest. The nuns and priests said you must be on the alert to see if you had the "calling" to a religious life. God would send you an internal message or you'd just know. Or you'd get a fortune cookie that said, "Become a priest." (Just kidding.)

The America I grew up during the 1950s did not seem so poisonously oppositional. The Republicans who voted for Dwight D. Eisenhower as president were not that radically different from the Democrats who had wanted Adlai Stevenson to win. Somehow the whole country could accept Eisenhower.

To me he seemed like a friendly grandfather. And, of course, he had been an admired general in World War II.

The whole country came together for World War II. My mother was a WAVE during the war, my mother's brother Barry was in the Navy, my father's sister Sue was in the Coast Guard, his sister Dorothea (Dossie) was in the Army, stationed in England.

My father was also in the Army. He was in Ireland for a while. And then he was part of the D-Day invasion in Normandy. We were very proud of him for that, but it was not spoken of too much. (Not sure why. My father was somewhat reticent about it. Plus all the women in the family talked all the time. I have very talky women in my plays, you may notice. Such as Luella in *Why Torture Is Wrong, and the People who Love Them,* one of my favorite characters I've written recently.)

John Kennedy ran for president in 1960, and he was the second Catholic to run for the White House. The first was Al Smith in 1928, who lost to Herbert Hoover. The stock market crash that brought on the Depression happened in 1929, so at the time Hoover was popular. During Al Smith's candidacy, there was a fear that any Catholic president would have to "obey the pope." And it was known that Catholics believed the pope to be "infallible on matters of dogma and morality."

About papal infallibility, and recalling my having been taught that, I am agog with admiration for the various popes—I think declaring oneself to be infallible is the very, very best way to win all arguments. At age seven, though, I just accepted the pope's infallibility as a fact, since that's how it was presented. The sun is in the sky, the grass is green, the pope is infallible.

Anyway, as soon as Kennedy got the nomination to run for president, the "will he take his orders from the pope?" questions started up again. But it was now 1960 and Catholics were more integrated into American society. And Kennedy chose to specifically defuse the issue by giving a speech to the Greater Houston Ministerial Association where he declared:

> I believe in an America where the separation of church and state is absolute—where no Catholic prelate would tell the President (should he be Catholic) how to act, and no Protestant minister would tell his parishioners for whom to vote . . .

> I believe in an America that is officially neither Catholic, Protestant nor Jewish—where no public official either requests or accepts instructions on public policy from the Pope, the National Council of Churches or any other ecclesiastical source—where no religious body seeks to impose its will directly or indirectly upon the general populace or the public acts of its officials—and where religious liberty is so indivisible that an act against one church is treated as an act against all.

I chose to include that second paragraph because I feel that in America many religious conservatives would not embrace the kind of separation Kennedy was describing then. The separation has been blurring.

As a schoolchild growing up among my middle-class family, the church-state separation I had heard of seemed to match Kennedy's words. Somewhere along the way I was taught that the Puritans came to American to avoid religious persecution; they were escaping societies where a dominant religion held sway. So in America they wanted to keep church and state separate, lest one religion or another might impose itself on others. Is that still taught? I bet it isn't.

But back to 1960 presidential campaign, my parents and the extended family did NOT vote for Kennedy, even though he was Catholic.

They voted for Richard Nixon because he had a long history of "fighting communism." (And also they liked his "cloth coat" speech, in which he got out of a scandal by saying his wife Pat didn't have much money and wore a simple "cloth coat".)

Fear of communism was the one political issue that I was aware of as a child. The nuns in school and the priests in Sunday sermons made it clear that the communists were atheists and that they would not let Catholics practice their religion.

We also were warned that communists might come from other countries and pass for Americans and then would infiltrate local governments and maybe national government too. And worst-case scenario, you could wake up one morning and discover you were now living in a communist state. AND you wouldn't be able to go to Catholic Mass or Catholic schools anymore.

So when I was six and seven, I was somewhat worried about this.

And we all were worried about the atom bomb, which Russia had, and if we were unlucky Russia would bomb us to smithereens. And later on we were worried that Russia or we ourselves might "hit the button" by mistake, and the whole world could blow up. (This was the theme of the brilliant satiric film *Dr. Strangelove, or How I Learned to Stop Worrying and Love the Bomb,* a film that had a hand in losing Barry Goldwater the 1964 election against Lyndon B. Johnson. To voters Goldwater seemed too open to pushing the button.)

But day-to-day life in an American suburb in New Jersey felt safe and calm. And I was mostly focused on musicals and screwball comedies from the 1930s.

There were only a few channels on TV, and most families watched *The Ed Sullivan Show,* a popular variety show on Sunday nights. He had famous singers and performers and also songs and scenes from current Broadway musicals. Thanks to that program and the smaller number of options for entertainment, theater really had a national profile in America—something that it no longer has, which makes me sad.

But inspired by *The Ed Sullivan Show,* I announced at age six that I wanted to sing "Chicago" at my aunt Phyllis's students' piano recital. Which I did. And when I was eight I wrote a two-page play, which surprisingly my second-grade class put on one afternoon during class time, with me casting and directing it. From then on, I kept writing plays. The next one was 10 pages, then 15, etc., etc. My most recent play was 5,687 pages long. I need to cut it some.

We didn't get a TV until I was four or five, so I never went through that watching-cartoons period.

Instead I watched old movies from the 1930s and 1940s. Sometimes I would be allowed to stay up to watch *I Love Lucy*. It truly felt like the whole country watched that show each week, and the hilarious Lucille Ball was much beloved. And since I watched all those old movies, I would marvel at seeing a young Lucille Ball show up in a bit part in the Astaire-Rogers 1936 film *Follow the Fleet*, and then later see her play a serious leading lady in the plane-crash-in-the-jungle movie *Five Came Back*. (She was one of the five who got out. Everybody else got eaten by cannibals.)

But politics weren't part of my childhood or early teens.

Then suddenly there was the Vietnam War.

The Vietnam War never "began," at least from my child viewpoint, but I think it snuck up on the whole country, not just me. At the end of the Kennedy administration, we had 16,000 troops in Vietnam (as advisers, and also pilots in bombing raids). After Kennedy's assassination, suddenly Vice President Lyndon Johnson was in charge, and in a fairly under-the-radar way he started increasing our troops substantially in Vietnam.

When I was fifteen, the Gulf of Tonkin Resolution was affirmed by the Senate and the Congress. This resolution was triggered by three North Vietnamese PT boats shelling a U.S. destroyer. The resolution allowed Johnson to do "anything" he felt he needed to in response to North Vietnamese aggression. And this resolution specifically allowed Johnson to NOT ask the Congress to declare war.

But I never heard any adult in my earshot say, "Oh, did you hear about the Tonkin Resolution today?" Or, "Wow, I guess that means we're committing to a war." But that's what had happened.

And suddenly by the time I was sixteen, we had many soldiers in Vietnam. And it was no volunteer army—every American male had to register for the draft and could be sent to Vietnam. My junior year in high school, the 16,000 American troops during the Kennedy administration had become 385,300. The next year 485,600. The year after that 536,100.

And unlike the clarity of how we got into World War II—with Hitler invading countries and Japan bombing Pearl Harbor—how and why we got into Vietnam was very fuzzy to most people.

For many, the mere words "we're fighting the communists" was enough.

My grandmother and my uncle Barry and the entertainer Bob Hope all said, "When your country tells you to go to war, you just go to war." Or in other words, "ours not to reason why, ours but to do and die." (The correct quote from the Lord Alfred Tennyson poem is actually "theirs not to reason why," but over time it has morphed into "ours," which is more immediate and more "this could happen to me.")

But it was a bloody, confusing war, and it was on TV nightly.

From the news one got that North Vietnam was communist and South Vietnam was not. And the North was trying to invade the South, and so Americans were over there trying to stop that.

But I learned a more complicated explanation in my high school. I went to a terrific Catholic high school taught by Benedictine monks. One of the younger monks taught us history, and a few of us hung out after class one day and asked about Vietnam.

Father Gregory told us background we had never heard in discussion or in TV. He explained that the Vietcong were not from the North but were South Vietnamese who sided with the communists. And Vietnam had been one country, but it had been split into two parts, and they were supposed to have held elections to put the country back together, but countries like the United States and others didn't want these elections because they feared Ho Chi Minh would win. So instead we were propping up a corrupt government. And there were enormous casualties on all sides.

At the same I had become a pacifist. I had befriended a fellow student named Beriau, who challenged me with the idea that Christ in the gospels actually wanted his followers to be pacifists, to turn our backs on violence. "Turn the other cheek." "Resist not the evildoer." "Love thy enemy." "Blessed are the peacemakers." Except for Christ's conniption fit with the money changers in the Temple, he did seem very nonaggressive and peaceful.

I have some sympathy with religious conservatives who feel convinced that they are right because I had that same feeling in my late teens that I was right in interpreting Christ as antiwar and in viewing the Vietnam War as a big, immoral mistake. (I say immoral because we were killing so many civilians in our bombing raids; and furthermore we had injected ourselves into what was basically a civil war.)

So I had a very buoyant two years where I felt in synch with a very liberal Christianity, and with knowing what direction the world must go in to survive.

I went to peace marches. Some of the younger monks marched in them too. The peace marches were mostly joyful, singing "I ain't gonna study war no more." The large New York City peace march in August 1967 was especially filled with good vibes, and people leaned out their office buildings cheering the marchers.

I went to college, bushy-tailed, energetic, and hopeful. Democratic senator Eugene McCarthy, the sole voice against the Vietnam War in Washington (or so it seemed), announced he would run against Lyndon B. Johnson, challenging his reelection bid. Those of us opposed to the war were ecstatic. We believed our movement would spread and spread. As the musical *Hair* said, "This is the dawning of Aquarius." As Bob Dylan said, "The times they are a-changin'."

Lo and behold, Johnson announced he was NOT going to run for a second term. We felt triumphant. Senator Robert Kennedy seemed a little late to the antiwar stance, but he announced plans to run for president, and now he too was against the war.

McCarthy got pushed aside due to Kennedy's fame. It seemed unfair, but, on the other hand, just electing someone who would end the war was the important thing.

Martin Luther King Jr. was a pastor and a world-changing civil rights leader. He was inspiring to blacks, but to many whites too. He also taught nonviolence. He and Mahatma Gandhi were the only famous people I knew who were pacifists. And Martin Luther King had come out against the war in Vietnam.

But the excitement and hope antiwar people felt was dashed. On April 4 Martin Luther King Jr. was assassinated. On June 18 Robert Kennedy Jr. was assassinated.

Martin Luther King's murder was devastating. In the freshman dining hall, whites and blacks often sat together. The morning after King's death, the black students sat apart from the white students. Who could blame them, but it was a noticeable switch. And it lasted a long time.

And then, with McCarthy marginalized and Kennedy dead, the presidential choice boiled down to Republican Richard Nixon versus Johnson's vice president, Hubert Humphrey. Most of us didn't expect Nixon to be back, but he was. And Nixon and Humphrey BOTH vowed to keep the Vietnam War going the same as Johnson: we must protect against that so-called domino effect, blah blah blah.

I went into a deep depression. The fact that our protests came so close to making a change in the Vietnam War, but then didn't—I gave up on politics at that point. I disengaged entirely.

To be honest, my depression was not due only to politics. I had my own demons to deal with—namely growing up in an alcoholic family, not just my father, but various aunts and uncles, and both of my grandfathers; and in the family, problems never, ever got solved, just endlessly repeated. And I also realized I was gay, which at the time I thought was depressing information, since "no gay person could ever be happy," as some early therapist told me. (I only saw him once. I found better ones later.)

I don't know if I would have voted for Humphrey—he seemed identical to Nixon on the war. But back then, the voting age was twenty-one, and in 1968 I was nineteen, so I could not vote anyway. The draft age was eighteen. You could die for your country, but you couldn't vote.

In the 1960s if you went to college, you automatically had a student deferment and would not be drafted until you finished college (or flunked out). But obviously I was aware I could eventually be sent to fight in the war.

My sophomore year Nixon was elected, and my junior year the draft suddenly switched to a lottery system instituted for young men born between 1944 and 1950. The lottery put the month and day of every possible birthday into a large glass bowl and then chose them randomly, numbering them 1 through 366 (including leap year). The lower numbers would be drafted immediately (unless still in college), and the higher numbers probably wouldn't be called. September 14 was the first birth date chosen (#1), and everyone with that birth date would be drafted almost immediately. June 8 was the 366th one chosen, and people with that birthday would not be drafted.

My handsome, popular-with-girls roommate Marty got the number 265 or something—very lucky. He could pretty much know he wouldn't be drafted.

I got the number 159. I recall being told that draft boards in 1969 were calling up to 180 or 190. I felt unlucky, but still safe with my student deferment.

To everyone's surprise, the virulently anticommunist Richard Nixon started to slowly de-escalate the war. When the lottery began, we had 475,200 troops in Vietnam. When I graduated in 1971, the troop levels had gone down to 156,800. I was told that draft boards were only calling up to the number 100. So I was not drafted.

Obviously people 100 and below were, and some, probably many, died. I literally had "the luck of the draw." I believed the Vietnam War to be a tragic error in judgment by our leaders, and I am glad I was not forced to fight in it. For those who did believe and who fought, they were honorable to do what they thought was right. But for the many who did not agree, it's a pretty existential position to go, "Oh, I think it's wrong, but I'll be a good sport and go kill and be killed due to uncles and grandmothers and Bob Hope."

In 1973 the draft came to an end. It was replaced by an all-volunteer army.

For the next many years I paid little attention to politics. An exception was the Nixon scandal nicknamed Watergate was inescapable, and fascinating. (And this scandal triggered the weird adding of "gate" to the end of every other scandal name for the next several decades: Monicagate, travelgate, nannygate, troopergate. If only Bill Gates would have a scandal, we could have Gatesgate.)

In 1971 I was lucky indeed to get into Yale School of Drama as a playwright. The teachers and fellow students were exciting. From then until about age thirty-six, I wrote prolifically. I had been shy and withdrawn in college, but I became semi-outgoing and ambitious suddenly.

Started at Yale, my 1977 play *A History of the American Film* was one of my few early plays that had a political component to it. The plot was a mad dash through American history and American "self-image," and dealt with Prohibition, censorship (the production code), World War II, the "internment" of Asian Americans during the war, the atom bomb, and the postwar period. But it also was a romp, celebrating the movies I saw as a child and so loved.

(The play somewhat grew out of an independent study I did in college with Doris Kearns Goodwin, where I researched the box office successes of the 1950s and the 1960s and analyzed how the 1960 films became darker and darker in comparison to the sunny and/or religious ones of the 1950s. Ms. Kearns was an inspiring associate professor back then, and had not yet married Richard Goodwin.)

But in most of my plays I wrote about "life"—family, child-parent stuff, drinking, how hard it is to be alive—kind of absurdist existentialism.

And the old adage "Write about what you know" obviously includes your family, your upbringing, your relationships, etc., etc. But also your religion, especially if you had a strong connection to it.

And I was influenced and inspired by how frequently the playwright Joe Orton and the filmmaker Federico Fellini included their Catholic upbringing in their work. So at Yale, from time to time, I would bring in Catholic characters or themes—usually not at the center of the play, though.

In spring 1976 my mother had a recurrence of cancer, and the prognosis was not hopeful. With chemo and radiation, she hung in there about three years, and most of the time, alas, it was physically and psychologically painful for her. People look to their faith to find comfort during sickness and fear of death. As much as I wished I could believe my childhood religion, I was unable to. However, I certainly supported my mother's finding comfort in the Church's teaching of heaven and life everlasting. At my mother's funeral, a priest who had met her either never or once claimed that she had illuminated how to handle death. I think that was ludicrous to say. I think my mother was perfectly normal and found impending death unexpected and unwanted.

My mother's illness made me look back at what I had been taught, and while she was still alive I started to write a play that eventually became *Sister Mary Ignatius Explains It All for You.*

The Catholic teaching of my youth had an explanation for absolutely everything, and so the "explains it all for you" part of the title was very important to me.

I only wrote the beginning of the play and then put it aside. It was not an easy time to write; I was spending a lot of time with my mother, and her doctors, and I also found the squabbling between her and her family to be exhausting. They all meant well (well, maybe my uncle Barry didn't), but that family of my mother's sure liked to argue! (My grandmother always took sides when her children fought, and this was a hideous recipe for making everyone bicker and fight all the time.)

My mother got to see my play *A History of the American Film* on its opening night on Broadway on March 30, 1978. On March 10, 1979, she died. She was fifty-six.

I went back to writing, and I finished *Sister Mary Ignatius.* When Sister's ex-students showed up to playfully interrupt her lecture, I surprised myself where the play went. When the angry student Diane began to talk about the death of her mother, a large section of what she said was triggered by my mother—chiefly when she woke from a coma for several seconds and looked at me with utter horror, as if to say, "Can't you stop this from happening?" I don't mean it was blaming, it was just that I saw her panic and shock and fear, and it was painful to witness.

People often assume I based Sister Mary on a specific person. I did not. I went to Catholic schools for twelve years (first grade through twelfth). I was taught by nuns, whom I thought were good teachers, if sometimes grouchy, and by Benedictine monks whom I found smart and who treated their students as young adults.

So I wasn't upset with any specific nuns actually. I was upset with the dogma. As a child, I viewed the teachings as fact. In my late teens I stopped believing. In my twenties I found it hard not to have a religious belief, but after a while I stopped thinking about it. And when I was thirty, I started to look back at what I was taught, and was amazed that it now seemed highly debatable and, from a distance, kind of humorous.

For instance, an unbaptized baby who died couldn't go to heaven but could only go to "Limbo" and "could never see God." God apparently required the sacrament of baptism.

Or the odd rule that if you ate meat on Friday instead of fish or peanut-butter-and-jelly sandwiches, you would go to hell. Christ died on the cross on Friday, and we needed to commemorate this by not eating meat.

Or all the sexual teachings forbidding any sexual behavior outside of marriage. The wording for children in the catechism forbade "all impure acts alone or with others." "Alone" meant masturbation, I realized later. Thus Hitler is in hell for exterminating millions of Jews, and a thirteen-year-old boy is in hell for masturbation. It makes God sound crazy, doesn't it?

If God exists—which I can't tell, but am open to it—I do not think he/she/entity is crazy. Do you?

I think human beings have made up crazy rules that make life hard for people, and then they CLAIM these rules come from God. And they are wrong. They often are sincere in their belief, but if I can realize that the pope most likely is NOT infallible, I would like it if the more emphatic religious people would question the wisdom of trying to force others to follow rules based on their interpretation of God.

Sister Mary Ignatius was an unexpected audience and critical success. Initially it ran for only three weeks at Ensemble Studio Theater, but it got me much notice and I won an 1980 Obie award for playwriting.

In 1981, André Bishop at Playwrights Horizons re-presented the play, this time with a curtain raiser I wrote called *The Actor's Nightmare*. This version kept the same director—the wonderful Jerry Zaks—and the same actress as Sister Mary Ignatius—the wonderful Elizabeth Franz (who had won an Obie for her portrayal in the EST production). Lightning struck twice, and the reviews were once again terrific. The play moved to off-Broadway and ran for two and a half years. Other theaters around the country (in L.A., San Francisco, Boston, Chicago) produced the play.

Suddenly I was making a living as a playwright, which is hard to do, and it was thrilling for me. Due to my higher writing profile, I also suddenly could get screenwriting assignments.

So the success of *Sister Mary Ignatius* was a boon for me. And I had a hit play running in New York.

But suddenly there were protests against the play: picketing; people wanting the play to be canceled or shut down.

It began in St. Louis. I first heard of it when *Variety* wrote about it on December 1, 1982:

> The old time specter of censorship, thought to be as extinct as dinosaurs, has arisen here.
>
> The Theater Project Co.'s planned January production of *Sister Mary Ignatius Explains It All for You* has been publicly attacked by Archbishop L. May and by the local chapter of the Catholic League for Religious and Civil Rights, with the latter group calling for a ban on the production.
>
> At the same time, the Gateway Hotel, announced several months ago as the site, has discovered "technical difficulties" that will preclude the leasing of the space for *Sister Mary Ignatius*.
>
> Frances Noonan, president of the local chapter of the Catholic League, said her organization had two objectives, the first being "to halt the production. If the play is produced, we'd like to halt future public funding for the Theater Project Co."
>
> . . . there has been no overt attempt to legislate morality in the St. Louis theater since 1970, when the late Doris Bass urged fellow members of the Board of Aldermen to ban *Hair.* Her attempt did not succeed.

The play did go on in St. Louis, but there were ongoing complications and repercussions. First, the hotel discovered these sudden "technical difficulties," and two nearby universities offered their theater space to the company, in a gesture of supporting free speech. One, Washington University, was a private university; the other, the University of Missouri, was publicly funded.

A state senator got involved—Senator Edwin L. Dirck, a Democrat and chairman of the Appropriations Committee. He called in Arnold B. Grobman, the chancellor of the University of Missouri, demanding he defend his choice of letting an "anti-Catholic" play to be done on publicly funded property.

Mr. Grobman said he had allowed the Theater Project to use space at the university in the past and explained, "I don't tell them what plays to perform any more than I tell teachers what to teach or students what to read." He added that he didn't find the play anti-Catholic but rather "a satire on parochial education."

Senator Dirck was quoted in the papers as saying that Mr. Grobman had offended every person on the committee and he threatened budgetary reprisals.

Senator Dirck was equally upset with the head of the Missouri Arts Council, Talbot McCarthy. Dirck warned her that if she did not condemn the Theater Project for this "anti-Catholic" play and did not immediately rescind the grant that the theater had received, then the Arts Council funding might be in jeopardy.

Ms. McCarthy said she was sorry for offending anyone but that the grants were based on past work of the various theaters and that "our role is not to censor every work by the 500 groups we support."

I want to say here that almost every theater in the country has some sort of tax funding in it—the nonprofit regional theaters, even community theaters. Only the "for profit" Broadway and off-Broadway production have no tax money in them. So forbidding production of a play or musical that offended some people could have major repercussions for authors and audiences both. And what is available to be seen could end up being controlled by society's most easily offended citizens.

An odd fact was that though the Theater Project indeed had received a tax-supported grant, not a single penny of it had gone to the production of *Sister Mary Ignatius* (whose run had now completed). The Arts Council grant was only 3 percent of the Theater Project's budget; but the Arts Council had not given the grant money BEFORE the production; they always gave the money AFTER the Theater Project sent in receipts for reimbursement. However, the controversy made the play a big financial success. So the play made a profit, and no reimbursement was going to be asked for from the Arts Council. Just a quirk, but it gives a sense of the complexity of all of this.

The story went national. The *New York Times* did an article. On TV it was on the *Charles Kuralt CBS News Sunday Morning, Entertainment Tonight,* and *The Phil Donahue Show*. After the latter, the box office for *Sister Mary Ignatius* soared in New York and Los Angeles.

I was shocked I was being called "anti-Catholic" and "bigoted." I mean, I was TAUGHT all those things in Catholic school. It's my personal background. And if I disagree with a lot of the teaching, well, is that surprising? Lots of people do, and lots don't. And I am not talking about a RACE of people. I am talking about a belief system. And I find that the belief system is often illogical and sometimes damaging. My play is an unusual discussion and satire of the religious ideas imparted to me from age six on. It is not "bigoted."

Over the life of my play *Sister Mary Ignatius,* I have found that it is often viewed gratefully by lapsed Catholics. And more secure believing Catholics can accept the play as criticism and agree with much of it, even all of it. When the Jewish Anti-Defamation League, first in St. Louis and then in Boston, joined the protests against my play (including on TV), I was offended. The play is my reaction to my own religious teaching. How dare they decide they have standing to claim my view of the Church is wrong and/or "bigoted"? (Though they're probably just afraid of religions being criticized in general; and I somewhat understand that.)

The protests continued in other cities. In Boston before it even opened, it was condemned by the mayor and the bishop. There was much picketing, though once the good reviews came out, disagreeing with the protests, it calmed down. Then in Detroit a production was canceled. In Ponca City, Oklahoma, another production was canceled after a local priest called *Sister Mary Ignatius* anti-Catholic bigotry, but complained that the theater's previous production of *Man of La Mancha* was also bigoted, citing its mentions of the Spanish Inquisition. The Catholic Church tortured people during the Spanish Inquisition, but I guess it's bigoted to mention it.

I kept hearing from all these theaters. In Erie, Pennsylvania, a production was almost canceled, until the local press revealed that the director was a Polish émigré who came to America looking for "artistic freedom." People felt embarrassed about the émigré finding his first project about to be shut down, and so everyone changed their minds, and that production went on after all.

In Coral Gables, Florida, I got a phone call from the happy people presenting the play. They had a success on their hands. The local bishop and the city council had condemned the play in advance, but then the production promptly sold out to laughing crowds. They did tell me that the theater received three bomb threats, though they didn't seem scared about it. I found it scary.

I recall one day going to my dentist who said, "Did you see the editorial against you in the paper today?" I didn't know what he was referring to, but it turned out that the *New York Post* had a nationally syndicated column written by Patrick Buchanan condemning the play and quoting someone who said the play was the most vile piece of anti-Catholic bigotry he had ever seen. (Buchanan clearly hadn't seen it, so he quoted someone else.)

Partially it was exciting to write a play that got such a large reaction.

One of the recurring themes in all of my plays, including the early absurdist ones, is the very forceful person who bullies other people and insists on getting his or her way.

It's one thing to decry my play as something you don't like. It's another to try to actually keep the play from being seen or produced.

The *Sister Mary Ignatius* controversies went on and on for a few years. And then other plays and movies were similarily attacked. Looking back, it's clear to me that these protests were the beginning of the aptly named Culture Wars.

Martin Scorsese's film *The Last Temptation of Christ* was called anti-Catholic by the Catholic League and other conservative groups, and it was picketed.

A wonderful movie called *Priest* was protested by the Catholic League and its followers, who often came out to picket, it seemed. The movie was extremely Christian, I thought, but it was definitely critical of the Church's highly debatable rule of imposing celibacy on its priests and nuns. The League found discussing these issues to be anti-Catholic bigotry. A theater in Madison, New Jersey, showed the film and received a bomb threat. The theater stopped showing the film.

Terrence McNally wrote a play called *Corpus Christi*, named for his birth town in Texas. In the play a group of gay actors put on a play about Christ on earth. It was protested as blasphemous and anti-Catholic. The protestors, based on a faulty *New York Post* column, believed the play said Christ was gay. It did not. It was actually kind of religious; it just showed a troupe of gay actors acting out the Bible story of Christ. The New

York theater got bomb threats, and for the rehearsals and performances, everyone in the theater had to go through a bomb detector system.

It's odd: all these bomb threats I've mentioned preceded our terrorist attack on 9/11. I hope Americans who don't like certain books, plays, and movies will grow up and allow for difference of opinion, and not try to win dominance for their beliefs by shutting up others with bomb threats (or actually setting off bombs).

Since those attacks on my play and others, I have been sensitized to forceful religious people who impose their beliefs on the entire country (or world). Opposition to birth control (including family planning in foreign countries). Opposing stem cell research. The cardinals (and others) who claimed that condoms didn't protect against AIDS. Gay rights made great strides over the past years, but opponents claim tolerance/acceptance of gays is "social engineering." And it's all based on their religious interpretations. You remember that antigay speech Jesus gave, right? "Blessed are the peacemakers. But for God's sake, condemn gay people."

This is a lighter anecdote, but I remember learning about blue laws when I lived in Connecticut as a grad student. It was 1972 and I was in a children's show at Yale, and before the Sunday performance I stopped at a drugstore to buy tissues to help with putting on my makeup. I was playing the evil Baroness's troll, and the Baroness was played by my fellow student Sigourney Weaver.

But the store wouldn't sell me tissues on a Sunday because of Connecticut's blue laws, which forbade selling anything nonessential on a Sunday because Sunday was God's day. I said to the person behind the counter, "I can't buy tissues? I'm about to go perform for an audience of children. Do you want them to be disappointed if I'm not made up properly in my troll makeup?"

Obviously I was being amused at the oddness of it. I'm sure Sigourney would loan me tissues—she's a very generous person. However . . . though that's more of a silly example, I really feel we must avoid putting people's religious views into law.

As a playwright I don't write politically all the time. I have lots of family stuff and life-is-hard stuff that inspires me, but I am also made angry by forceful people imposing their will on others. And for that reason, I do find myself writing about political things.

There are a bunch of short political plays in this volume. They are very short, and I wrote them scattershot over many years.

An Altar Boy Talks to God was triggered by the religious leaders who said that AIDS was God's punishment of gay people. *Cardinal O'Connor* is about the Catholic Church's obsessive and illogical opposition to birth control, juxtaposed with the Church's making all sorts of exceptions to "thou shalt not kill" (namely in war, which over history the Church has usually embraced). *Entertaining Mr. Helms* is a sketch that envisions a family that Senator Jesse Helms would approve of. *The Doctor Will See You Now* was triggered by the need to contact the sexual partners of people with AIDS (which I understood), but I blurred it in my mind with the "parental consent laws" and did an absurdist take on an intrusive government out of control.

Under Duress: Words on Fire was filmed by PBS. I played myself, my friend Kristine Nielsen played a friend, and it was about worries about global warning. It was filmed in 1990. Isn't it nice to know we're still arguing if global warning/climate change actually exists twenty-one years later. Maybe when we're all dead we can find out. My "character" discusses writing a letter to President Bush—it is the FIRST President Bush. There were two of them. But perhaps you know that.

I have also included *The Hardy Boys and the Mystery of Where Babies Come From,* which is not remotely political. It's short and very silly and is performed in high schools a lot. So I've included it just for fun.

My favorite of the short political plays is *The Book of Leviticus Show.* I wrote it in 1978 or 1979, I can't quite remember. It was triggered by singer Anita Bryant's 1977 antigay campaign called *Save the Children.*

Ms. Bryant, who had seemed a pleasant enough singer and was best known for her orange juice ads, burst onto the news in opposition to an antidiscrimination bill that had passed in Dade County, Florida. Ms. Bryant fought to overturn this bill, and she was on the national news saying that homosexuality was sinful and that homosexuals must never teach children (of any age) because homosexual "recruit" children. All homosexual teachers must be fired.

Ms. Bryant quoted the book of Leviticus as her biblical proof that God was opposed to homosexuality. Leviticus is in the Old Testament, and I had never read it. When I read it, I was appalled. IT IS INSANE. It is a list of "don'ts" and begins with the Jewish dietary rules, which Christians ignore. It also says that "men who lie with men" should be put to death, but goes on to say all adulterers should be put to death as well.

The idea anyone used this crackpot part from the Bible enraged me, and still does. And so I wrote *The Book of Leviticus Show* in response. The late 1970s was at the beginning of public access TV, in which all sorts of "regular people" could put themselves on TV. (In New York City at the time, it was absolutely fascinating. It's been taken over by YouTube now.)

So my main character was a friendly, sincere, but loony lady who had her own public access show; and each week she tried to "follow" the book of Leviticus.

Many more people saw Ms. Bryant than saw my play, of course.

Ms. Bryant was unrelenting and toxic on the national stage, and she SUCCEEDED in repealing the antidiscrimination law. It was the most public outburst against homosexuals I had seen in my life. And in 1986 in *Bowers v. Hardwicke* the Supreme Court ruled 5-4 that states could criminalize people for consensual homosexual relations. And their main "legal" argument was that condemnation of homosexual acts was in the Bible, and people had followed it for centuries. In other words, if it was good enough for Oscar Wilde to be sent to prison, well, let's not tinker with something that's working.

Hmmm. Separation of church and state? I was appalled; and I think Ms. Bryant's outbursts were a kind of "homosexual culture war," following an ongoing beginning acceptance of gay characters in American culture. (I actually think the Michael York bisexual-but-mostly-gay character in the 1972 movie *Cabaret* was the beginning of more sympathetic views of homosexuals. They didn't always kill themselves anymore.)

In 2003 the Supreme Court heard *Lawrence v. Texas* and in a 5 to 4 decision (again) overturned *Bowers v. Hardwicke,* finding that the state lacked a legitimate interest in regulating the private sexual conduct of consenting adults. Justice Antonin Scalia, a Catholic and the most conservative member of the Court, said that the majority was "signing on to the so-called homosexual agenda."

Yes, imagine letting people do what they want in their bedrooms. I cannot imagine it. I want to know what Justice Scalia does in his bedroom, and legally stop him from it. And if he does nothing in his bedroom, I want to legally *force* him to have sex of some kind. And I also want to know what he eats, and I want to impose my eating habits on him. I hope he likes ginger ale and Entenmann's cakes.

In recent years I wrote two pieces with zero political content: *Mrs. Bob Cratchit's Wild Christmas Binge* and the musical *Adrift in Macao* (with music by Peter Melnick).

However, *Sex and Longing,* in 1994, was definitely political, especially regarding the blurring of the separation of church and state that I was harping on above. Writing the play, I was trying to write an epic, but it was a bit lopsided. I had two themes—sexual addiction and the (you've heard me before) forcing of other people's religious beliefs into the law. When the two topics intertwined, the play worked, I thought. Sometimes the two themes were stranded from each other. I keep thinking of how to rewrite it. But I wanted to include some scenes from it, because I think they're funny.

Betty's Summer Vacation, written in 1999, is a satire with a political component. I'm examining and satirizing how we get obsessed following certain news stories that turn into long-running and humiliating soap operas. I'm thinking of the Clarence Thomas/Anita Hill hearings, and then of course Bill Clinton and Monica Lewinsky, which wasted about two years of our national life. My play, though, uses more the examples of the gruesome murders represented by the Menendez brothers and also Lorena Bobbitt cutting off her husband's penis and throwing it into a field. Strangely, policemen found the severed penis, doctors reattached it, and oddly Mr. Bobbitt later made a porno film. For those of you who don't know the Bobbitt story (prominent when I was writing the play), I am not kidding about any of the story.

Miss Witherspoon in 2005 is more fanciful than political, but it has a slight political tinge to it. The play is about a woman disappointed in life and scared of things outside her control, and she has committed suicide.

In the netherworld she finds that she is slated to be reincarnated, but she refuses to go back. Sometimes she manages to stop the reincarnation; at other times, she indeed is reincarnated against her will and does her best to commit suicide again, including once as a six-week-old infant. During some of these unhappy returns to life, she learns of terrorism and severe climate change. Eventually she decides to face her various reincarnations, though she makes a special agreement to go back in time so she can impact the future for the better.

My most recent play is *Why Torture Is Wrong, and the People Who Love Them,* and it is definitely a political play. I had great fun writing it, though, and I feel it is ebullient rather than angry or depressing. I had two audience comments that delighted me.

The first was a thirty-five-ish man who came up to me after the matinee and said he was so grateful, he felt that I had encapsulated the entirety of what living through the George W. Bush presidency felt like, and he felt enormous relief for having had it comically reflected back to him.

The other was just a nice comment that came at an unusual time. I had just finished a conversation with someone who forcefully was telling me that she didn't like the ending. I did, but I felt gloomy about her comments.

I went to the subway, and in the subway car I noticed a woman of fifty or so, tall, who seemed to recognize me. She smiled, and I nodded. (I don't get recognized often, but sometimes.) She then came over to me and said, "I loved your play!" And I said, "Thank you!" She said, "And I especially liked the ending!"

I felt the universe or luck was sending me a nice message. I liked the woman on the subway more than I liked the woman who had harangued me.

Isn't it good we don't try to pass laws saying which person's opinion on my play's ending is correct?

I hope you enjoy the plays.

Christopher Durang
April 2012

Why Torture Is Wrong, and the People Who Love Them

Why Torture Is Wrong, and the People Who Love Them received its world premiere at The Public Theater (Oskar Eustis, artistic director; Andrew D. Hamingson, executive director) in New York City on April 6, 2009. It was directed by Nicholas Martin; the set design was by David Korins; the costume design was by Gabriel Berry; the lighting design was by Ben Stanton; the music was by Mark Bennett; the sound design was by David Levy; and the production stage manager was Stephen M. Kaus. The cast was as follows:

Felicity	Laura Benanti
Zamir	Amir Arison
Luella	Kristine Nielsen
Leonard	Richard Poe
Reverend Mike	John Pankow
Hildegarde	Audrie Neenan
Voice/Narrator	David Aaron Baker

CHARACTERS

FELICITY
A perfectly nice young woman of 25 to 34.

ZAMIR
A charismatic but mysterious young man of indeterminate ethnicity; dark-haired, probably Pakistani or Egyptian or Indian. But could look Italian or Greek too. Does not have an accent, sounds American, 25 to 39.

LUELLA
Felicity's mother, sweet, somewhat dazed/befuddled woman. Dresses well. Late 40s to mid-50s.

LEONARD
Felicity's father. Strong-minded, formidable, 100 percent sure he's right about everything. Late 40s to late 50s.

REVEREND MIKE
A minister who directs porno movies. Late 30s to late 40s. Likable face, bit sexy, mildly debauched feeling, like a Mickey Rourke or a Kevin Spacey.

HILDEGARDE
A conservative, old-fashioned woman in her mid-40s to late 50s. Admires Leonard greatly, has a crush on him, though she doesn't think of it that way to herself. A nice, neat hairdo. Maybe a navy blue skirt, a navy blue jacket, a white blouse, and pearls. Ladylike.

VOICE/NARRATOR
Age anywhere from late 20s to early 40s. Well-spoken, must make announcements. Also plays Looney Tunes (a hyperactive spy) and the suave Maitre d'. Maitre d' should sing well or pleasantly.

ACT I

Scene 1

A bedroom in a motel. A MAN *and woman asleep in bed. Man is in underwear and T-shirt and has dark hair. Woman is in a slip. Her name is* FELICITY.

Felicity wakes first. Disoriented. She has no idea where she is. Looks over at the man. He's still asleep. She gasps—she has no idea who he is. She peers closer—no, no idea.

She decides to quietly sneak out of the room. Finds her dress, starts to put it on.

Note: When a character strings two or more sentences together, separated only by commas, it is meant to indicate the character is speaking quickly or speedily. To an actor, a period suggests a stop. So the use of the commas in this ungrammatical way is meant to indicate the sentences and thoughts are somehat rushed, and there are no real stops in what is being said.

MAN Hey, how'd you sleep?

FELICITY Fine. Thank you.

MAN I was so drunk!

FELICITY Really. That's too bad. How do you feel now?

MAN My head hurts, but I'm used to that.

FELICITY Uh-huh. Was . . . was I drunk too?

MAN Were you drunk too??? (*laughs*)

FELICITY Yes, that's my question.

MAN Oh, well, I'm just repeating it because . . . wow . . . you were SO drunk. I mean "*Apocalypse Now*" kind of drunk. You were dancin' like crazy, then you'd throw up, then you'd dance like crazy, and you'd throw up again. It was . . . kinda hot.

FELICITY (*baffled why it's hot*) Really?

MAN Well not the vomit. I may have my kinky side—as you know. (*He looks at her knowingly; she looks blank, and worried.*) But it doesn't include regurgitation. I just meant the crazy abandon of it. That's what was hot.

FELICITY I see. Well, I'm glad you had a good time. Maybe we'll do it again someday. Do you know where my shoes are? I really should be going.

MAN Going? I mean . . . going?

FELICITY Well, I have a feeling I may have appointments. My brain isn't working yet, but I think I should get to my apartment.

MAN Well, usually married people live together, no?

She stares at him.

FELICITY What do you mean?

MAN I'm just saying normally married people live together.

FELICITY (*screams*) *AAAAAAAAAGGGGHHHH.*

MAN What's the matter?

FELICITY Are you saying we got married last night?

MAN Yeah. In between all the vomiting. You said you never put out unless you got married first. And I thought you were joking, but I decided to call your bluff. And we got married. See . . . (*shows her a ring on his finger*)

FELICITY Oh my God. (*looks at her hand*) But I don't have a ring.

MAN We got mugged on the way into the hotel.

FELICITY Were we hurt?

MAN I don't remember. I think you need to call and stop your credit cards, though.

FELICITY You mean my bag is gone?

MAN Yeah, that's what I mean.

FELICITY Did they take *your* credit cards?

MAN I don't have any. I'm . . . footloose and fancy free.

FELICITY Uh-huh. And you don't have any credit cards?

MAN I don't have good credit. I don't like to pay bills. Plus I think food and electricity and housing should be free.

FELICITY Do you have a job?

MAN Um . . . well, depends what you mean by a job.

FELICITY I mean, do you work and get paid?

MAN I'm not sure what you mean.

FELICITY Good God, if we're married, do you have any money? Do I have to earn everything?

MAN It would be great if you earned everything. I should have asked you last night, but thanks for offering it now.

FELICITY I'm not offering it, I'm just trying to figure out . . .

MAN Hey, I do stuff. Sometimes I drive a big van in the middle of the night, and I deliver things, and I get paid. Or I get a tip from someone where I can . . . you know, score something big. And sometimes I just find money . . . under a rock, you know.

FELICITY Under a rock?

MAN Yeah, I do something for somebody, it's a little dangerous, maybe a little illegal; and they tell me to go to some field and look for a tree by a rock, and underneath the rock there's this envelope with like, you know, a lotta cash.

FELICITY Oh, I'm feeling scared. Am I an alcoholic? Did I have a blackout? Did you give me a date rape drug?

MAN You mean like penicillin?

FELICITY No, I mean roofies or something.

MAN Roofies. (*laughs*) Baby, I don't need to give anybody roofies to go to bed with them.

FELICITY Well . . . is there . . . paperwork on this marriage?

MAN I think so. Hold on.

FELICITY If only I'm dreaming, and I can wake up.

MAN That's a hurtful thing to say. I have a temper, you know, be careful. (*goes through a pile of his clothes, finds something underneath*) Here it is. (*hands her something folder-like*)

FELICITY (*takes it*) It's a menu.

MAN Yeah, the marriage certificate is inside.

FELICITY (*opens it*) Ah. So it is.

MAN See. I told you.

FELICITY (*looks at menu*) Did we get married at Hooters?

MAN No. That's where you threw up the first time. But Hooters told us of this minister guy who also makes porno. And he married us.

FELICITY Also makes porno. I've never met anyone who makes porno.

MAN Yeah, that's what you said last night. I hope you're not going to repeat yourself a lot in our marriage. That would be a drag.

FELICITY Well, it's obvious we should get this annulled.

Man darkens, gets really mad.

MAN (*vicious, scary*) Who the fuck do you think you're talking to? Get this annulled? You think I'm a refrigerator you can just send back to Sears?

FELICITY Refrigerator?

MAN I may have been drunk, but I gave a lot of thought to asking you to marry me. I've never been married. I said to myself, Zamir, it's about time you got married. (*to her again*) You said you liked me last night, don't "diss" me by sayin' you want an annulment. I mean, do you wanna keep your teeth? You want your lungs to keep workin'?

FELICITY Oh my God. Okay, I see your point, don't get angry. And what about Zamir? Is your name Zamir?

ZAMIR Yeah. It's Irish.

FELICITY (*choosing not to argue*) Okay. Oh my. You see, I just don't remember last night, not the marriage, not the sex, assuming there was sex, and of the sex I don't remember, I don't remember anything that was kinky. How do you define kinky?

ZAMIR Oh baby, I'll define it for you again tonight.

FELICITY I mean, I don't know if you mean slightly kinky or truly disgusting.

ZAMIR Oh, baby, talk dirty to me.

FELICITY Look, I don't even remember meeting you. I really think we should get an annulment.

He makes angry sound and motion.

Or what about a trial separation?

ZAMIR God, you're making it worse and worse. I should tell you, my male ego is fragile, and when it gets bruised I can get violent. It's a flaw in my character, but all the women in my family are dead.

FELICITY What?

ZAMIR No, they're not dead. But they can tell you, I can get violent. Definitely don't use your good china at dinner with me.

FELICITY Okay, thanks for the tip.

ZAMIR When can I meet your parents?

FELICITY Um. How about never? Is never good for you?

He looks violent again.

No, I'm kidding. How about . . . this afternoon? I'll call them right up.

ZAMIR Oh, that's the gal I married. Give me a kiss. (*He goes to kiss her, she pulls away.*)

FELICITY We should really brush our teeth.

ZAMIR Ooooooh, kinky.

She looks confused.

Scene 2

A living room. Felicity comes into the room with purpose and sees her mother, LUELLA. *Luella is nicely dressed and is staring off in the distance, or maybe arranging flowers.*

FELICITY Hi. It's me.

LUELLA Darling, how lovely to see you.

FELICITY Thanks. Good to see you. Where's Daddy?

LUELLA He's upstairs with his butterfly collection.

FELICITY You know when I told my therapist about Daddy, he asked me if Daddy's butterfly collection was a euphemism.

LUELLA Well, I'll have to ask your father sometime.

FELICITY Mother, I have some news.

LUELLA How is the city, darling? Are you still enjoying the culture, the nightlife, the museums, the theater?

FELICITY Ecccch, I hate theater. It's so boring. It's just unbearable.

LUELLA Really? I enjoyed *Wicked.* Did you see it? It's about this green girl and she learns how to fly.

FELICITY No, I don't like going to the theater.

LUELLA Oh, are you referring to those three evenings of Tom Stoppard plays? There's a woman in my bridge club who said she knew someone who killed themselves during the third one, it was so dull.

FELICITY How did they kill themselves?

LUELLA I think it was force of will. They forced their heart to stop beating.

FELICITY You know, I'm reminded this is why I left home, we can't get the conversation to move forward in a linear way. (*firm*) Now listen to me: I have news for you. I'm getting married.

LUELLA You are? How wonderful. When is the wedding? May I come?

FELICITY No, I said it wrong. I've GOTTEN married. I'm already married.

LUELLA Oh. And may I come?

FELICITY What? No, it's past tense, it's happened. I already got married.

LUELLA Why didn't you tell me?

FELICITY Well, I didn't know myself.

LUELLA What?

FELICITY I mean . . . Gosh what do I mean? I mean I only got married . . . "spur of the moment," and I just thought . . . I should tell you in person, and you're never home.

LUELLA I'm always home. Who did you marry, dear?

FELICITY Um . . . he's a . . . you know, I don't know what to say about him.

LUELLA What does he do for a living?

FELICITY You know, I asked him that too. And he refuses to say. (*She signals for her mother to come closer, lowers her voice.*) I don't want him to hear us.

LUELLA Who, dear?

FELICITY He's in the other room.

LUELLA Who is, dear?

FELICITY I have a funny feeling about him. I'm afraid he might be a terrorist. Or maybe he's in the Mafia. Or maybe he's bipolar. Or maybe he's a serial killer. Or maybe he's just a drug addict and alcoholic and out of prison on parole.

LUELLA Who are you talking about, dear?

FELICITY My husband, my husband, my husband!

Zamir comes in.

ZAMIR Hello. Did you call?

FELICITY Yes, Zamir, I did. This is my mother. Mother, this is that person I just told you about.

LUELLA Felicity tells me she's afraid you're a terrorist or in the Mafia or bipolar or a serial killer or a drug addict on parole. I hope she's mistaken. Is she?

ZAMIR It's a pleasure to meet you, Mrs. Ratzywatzy. Felicity tells me that you and her father are very wealthy, and you can set us up in a house, and set me up in a business. I don't have time to go to work in a regular way, but if you set it up right and give me enough starter money, I could hire people to oversee the business.

LUELLA Why did you call me Mrs. Ratzywatzy?

FELICITY I told him that was our last name. I was . . . hoping he wouldn't be able to find us if we . . . moved to Kentucky or something.

LUELLA Well, I like the name. Maybe we should adopt it.

FELICITY Oh my gosh, I forgot to cancel my credit cards.

ZAMIR I've cut the wires to all the telephones.

FELICITY (*shocked, looks at Luella as if she might speak*) Mother, be quiet.

LUELLA I didn't say anything.

FELICITY Zamir, why did you cut the wires to the telephone?

ZAMIR No, I was thinking of cutting them. You know, in case you tried to call someone to get our marriage annulled. Or if I decided to rob anybody, you might try to call the police. But I realized, none of that is going to happen right now, so there was no need to cut the telephone wires. Plus I couldn't find the right cutting tool. Are all the tools in the cellar, or are some in an outside shed or something?

FELICITY What?

ZAMIR (*to Luella*) Hello, Mrs. Ratzywatzy. I'm your new son-in-law, Zamir. It's so nice to meet you. Your daughter is a delightful person. I'm so lucky to have married her.

LUELLA Nice to meet you, Zamir.

ZAMIR What's your name?

LUELLA My name is Luella, but most people call me Mother.

ZAMIR Hello, Luella.

LUELLA How did you and my daughter meet?

ZAMIR We met at Hooters.

LUELLA And who is Hooters?

ZAMIR It's a chain of restaurants about big knockers.

LUELLA Hmmm. I don't understand, but I hope someday to meet this Hooters person. Tell me, Zamir, what do you do for a living?

ZAMIR I'm not really allowed to say.

LUELLA What?

FELICITY You see? He wouldn't tell me either.

ZAMIR Look, you—honor and obey and shut up, all right? How'd you like my fist down your throat? My male ego is fragile, don't say anything critical, I can get violent easily.

LUELLA Oh, how masculine. I'm very impressed.

ZAMIR Oh, good thing to say.

FELICITY (*suddenly sniffs*) Do I smell butterflies burning?

LUELLA (*sniffs the air*) I don't think so. It smells more like French toast.

Enter the father, LEONARD.

LEONARD I incinerated a group of squirrels that was trying to get in and destroy my butterfly collection. I was going to use my assault weapon, but I decided to use the napalm projector, and it burned them all up to little piles of black stuff.

LUELLA Oh, I guess it wasn't French toast. What a shame. I love French toast.

ZAMIR Are you Felicity's father?

LEONARD Who are you?

ZAMIR I'm your daughter's husband.

LEONARD I didn't give my permission.

ZAMIR I didn't ask for it.

LEONARD I say you're not my daughter's husband.

ZAMIR I say you're not her father.

LEONARD I say you're robbing this house, and I killed you in self-defense. (*He takes out a gun and aims it at Zamir.*)

FELICITY No, no, stop, stop!

LEONARD Mind your place, Daughter.

FELICITY Father, stop it. No more killing.

LEONARD I don't like this man.

LUELLA Darling, you killed the squirrels; maybe we should leave it at that.

Leonard puts down his gun.

LEONARD Consider yourself put on warning, young man.

ZAMIR (*to Felicity*) Wow, I thought you married me just out of a random impulse because you were drunk. But now that I meet your father, maybe you have a psychological pattern you're dealing with.

LEONARD What? Drunk?

ZAMIR Yeah! We met at Hooters drunk, and got blasted out of our minds, then we found some porno minister who married us, and then we got mugged, and now we've come around to meet the parents. How'd you like hearing that story?

LEONARD I will kill you. (*He takes out gun again.*)

ZAMIR You better be careful. I've booby-trapped the house, it could blow up if I just dial a certain number on my cell phone. (*He takes out cell phone.*)

LEONARD I'm willing for the entire house to blow up, so don't push me, Mohammed.

ZAMIR My name is Zamir, you fuck face, and it's Irish!

LEONARD Felicity, Luella, at the count of two run out of the house. Then I'm going to shoot this man dead and dive out the window before the house blows up.

FELICITY Stop, stop! This is ESCALATING! Stop escalating. I've made probably a bad marriage, but let's not have the house blow up because of it. Let's negotiate, let's pretend we're the United Nations, and let's try to learn to reason and talk with one another.

LEONARD Did you say something positive about the United Nations? (*He goes over to her, raises his hand as if to slap her, but doesn't.*) The United Nations is worthless. I won't have it spoken of positively in this house, do you understand?

LUELLA You know, I could make French toast.

ZAMIR What's French toast?

FELICITY You don't know? Are you not American?

ZAMIR I'm American. I'm not French. What's French toast?

LEONARD Don't speak disrespectfully to my daughter. I will shoot you dead.

ZAMIR I will blow up the house. (*He re-takes his cell phone out of his pocket.*)

FELICITY Stop, stop. Let's start this all over. The amount of testosterone charging out of the two of you is disgusting. Enough with men needing to kill and blow things up all the time.

LUELLA French toast is quite delicious, Zamir. You take bread, and you soak it in uncooked egg yolk, then you fry it in butter on a skillet, and then you serve it with delicious warm maple syrup.

LEONARD That sounds good. Maybe we should have it. And we can discuss all this upset later.

LUELLA Oh, good. That sounds good. Let's go into the kitchen "nook"—we have a nook, Zamir, I don't know if Felicity told you. And I'll make French toast. And we'll postpone these angry exchanges until we all have a nice full stomach, and with luck are feeling sleepy.

LEONARD Come on, Zamir, let me show you where the kitchen nook is.

ZAMIR *(a bit suspicious, but it's probably okay)* All right . . .

Zamir follows Leonard off to the kitchen nook.

LUELLA *(whispers to Felicity)* Darling, sometimes you have to DISTRACT men, rather than actually bringing up the United Nations.

FELICITY Oh. Okay.

LUELLA Now you make superficial conversation with them for a little bit, and I'll make the French toast.

SCENE 3

The kitchen nook. Cozy, but rather small, they have to sit kind of close together around a table. Felicity, Zamir, and Leonard are there. Luella is offstage. They have cups of coffee and glasses of orange juice.

LEONARD My favorite butterflies are the swallowtail butterflies in the Papilionidae family. *(to Zamir)* Do you know that family of butterfly?

ZAMIR No. I told you, I know nothing of butterflies.

LEONARD They are a thing of beauty. Like an ostrich or a Fabergé egg.

ZAMIR Yeah, but you keep them, dead, right? In a little frame with a tiny pin piercing their heart.

LEONARD They don't have hearts. And yes, it's true, they are dead. By keeping them dead I get to preserve how they look, and admire them. I like the little pin stuck in them. It holds them in place, it's like the wire on the back of a beloved painting, except it's in the front and it's like a tiny dagger.

FELICITY I hope you like the French toast, Zamir. Daddy, you like French toast, remember?

LEONARD I don't like the French ever since they refused to be among the coalition of the willing in our war on terror in Iraq.

ZAMIR Would you like my opinion of the war?

LEONARD I would not. But I will tell you mine.

FELICITY Please, no, let's go back to talking about butterflies, okay?

Anxious to keep things pleasant, she changes the topic and speaks to Zamir.

Daddy has never shown Mother or me his collection, but we assume he really has one. Do you, Daddy? Or does something else go on upstairs on the third floor that we don't know about?

LEONARD What did you say?

FELICITY Nothing. I was just saying because you haven't ever shown me or Mother your collection, one wonders if it's real.

LEONARD Are you calling me a liar?

FELICITY No, no. Please. Um. I'm just saying how honored I'd be to see it sometime. Please . . . tell us some more about it.

LEONARD My favorite butterflies are the swallowtail butterflies in the Papilionidae family. The most beautiful include the anise swallowtail, and the Canadian tiger swallowtail, and the eastern festoon and the giant swallowtail.

Pause; they hope he's finished.

And the pipevine swallowtail. And the Queen Victoria birdwing. I miss Queen Victoria. Now that was a monarch. Oh, and, of course, there's the monarch butterfly, and they're beautiful, I'm sure, but rather common.

Pause again; Zamir and Felicity exchange looks, hoping he's done.

And there's the Solomon Island birdwing. And the western tiger swallowtail. And the zebra swallowtail. Most exquisite.

ZAMIR Uh-huh. You know, we've been talking about butterflies for ten minutes now. I wonder if we could change the topic to something that wasn't so FUCKING BORING!

Leonard stands, takes his gun out, and aims the gun directly at Zamir's head. The gun actually touches the side of his head. Felicity looks scared.

LEONARD I'm reminding myself of the photo from Vietnam. Do you remember it? Some officer or other had a gun right to this gook's head, and minutes after the photo was taken the man's head was blown to smithereens.

FELICITY Father, please sit down.

Enter Luella, holding two plates.

LUELLA Oh dear. And the French toast is ready now. Leonard, could you please put the gun down, dear. We're going to have French toast, which you love and which Zamir has never had before. Isn't that correct, Zamir?

ZAMIR Yes, that's correct.

LEONARD I was just remembering that photo from the Vietnam War with the gun pointed at the head of that gook, right in the middle of the street. Do you remember that, Luella?

LUELLA I remember the one of the poor little girl running naked down the street after she was hit by napalm.

LEONARD Yes, that was a good one too. A lot of fine photos came out of the Vietnam War. We should have won that war, but cowardly liberals like our daughter were traitors to this country and forced us to withdraw.

FELICITY Father, I wasn't even born yet.

LEONARD And that damn Jane Fonda. I blame her for our not winning that war. Of all the evil people in the 20th century, there's Hitler and Stalin and Saddam Hussein and then there's Jane Fonda.

LUELLA You liked her in *Barbarella,* didn't you? You said so at the time.

LEONARD That preceded her treasonous trip to North Vietnam. Before she betrayed her country and all the American soldiers, and me personally.

LUELLA I don't see how Jane Fonda betrayed you personally, Leonard.

LEONARD Well, she did.

FELICITY Mother, tell Father to let Zamir alone.

LUELLA Leonard, why do you have the gun pointed at Zamir's head?

LEONARD I can't remember.

LUELLA Well, if you can't remember, then you certainly mustn't kill him over something you've forgotten. So please sit down, and let's have brunch.

Leonard moves the gun away from Zamir's head and sits down.

God, I hate the second amendment.

LEONARD It's the right to bear arms, woman. And to protect the hearth and home.

FELICITY What is the hearth exactly?

LEONARD Shut up. You were happy I had guns when our house was broken into by that group of criminals.

FELICITY Father, they were children, you shot at children.

LEONARD They entered without knocking. They were wearing masks.

FELICITY It was Halloween.

LEONARD Well, they were dressed very oddly. I thought they were Mexicans. You don't enter someone's house wearing masks, and then expect not to be shot at.

FELICITY Well, you don't enter this house and expect not to be shot at, I agree with that. You're very quiet, Zamir. And you look a little angry. Daddy takes some getting used to. I hope your mind isn't planning something, is it?

ZAMIR No. I am just biding my time.

FELICITY Biding your time 'til what, Zamir?

ZAMIR Nothing. Until I get to be friends with my new wife's parents. (*He smiles at them, speaks to Luella.*) May I say how lovely you look, Mrs. Ratzywatzy? May I thank you for the French toast, which I expect is delicious.

LUELLA Thank you, Zamir.

LEONARD What did he just say? Did he threaten us?

FELICITY No, he paid Mother compliments. Please, Daddy, just eat your French toast, all right?

LEONARD We must call it Freedom Toast.

LUELLA What?

LEONARD Remember, that congressman from Ohio, Bob Ney, renamed French fries as Freedom fries, to offer support to our troops. Well, today I name this concoction you've made Freedom Toast.

FELICITY I don't want to call it Freedom Toast. That sounds stupid.

LEONARD Jane Fonda opposes our war in Iraq as well, you know. Once a traitor, always a traitor.

LUELLA Oh, for God's sake, can we just eat the Freedom Toast in peace, and shut up about politics for a MINUTE, please????

LEONARD Okay. Sure, let's eat.

They sit in silence and eat the French toast.

LEONARD (*eating, makes approving noise*) Mmmmm.

FELICITY (*also eating, approving*) Mmmmmm.

ZAMIR Mmmmm.

LEONARD Mmmmmmm.

FELCITY Mmmmmmm.

ZAMIR Mmmmmmmm.

LEONARD Mmmmmmmm.

ZAMIR These are delicious, Mrs. Ratzywatzy.

LUELLA Thank you, Zamir.

VOICE They continue to eat the French toast. The tension has momentarily abated. Only Felicity hears the voice speaking. She holds her head, wondering if now she's hearing voices, and she may be going mad.

Felicity has heard the voice and holds her head, looks worried.

Scene 4

Felicity's apartment. She and Zamir enter. They sit on a small couch. At some point in the scene Zamir pours them both some Fresca.

VOICE Felicity reluctantly has brought her new stranger/husband to her apartment. She doesn't hear the voice this time. Sometimes she hears it; other times she doesn't.

FELICITY Did you just hear something?

ZAMIR No. Did you?

FELICITY No. I guess not.

She looks confused. She sort of heard something, but isn't sure.

ZAMIR (*looking around*) Well, I like your apartment. It's a little small, but it'll do until your parents buy us a house. And I could imagine living out in New Jersey like they do. Maybe a bit closer to Jersey City. I know various people in Jersey City.

FELICITY I don't think my father is going to buy you a house. He hates you.

ZAMIR He'll grow to love me. Everyone does.

FELICITY Do they?

ZAMIR Sure. It's a little small here. It's a bit like the kitchen nook. Do you and your family have a "small thing."

FELICITY "Small thing"? I don't know what you mean.

ZAMIR Don't you call my thing small.

FELICITY What?

ZAMIR Nothing. Making a joke to myself. I do that from time to time.

FELICITY I see. Um, Zamir. Come here.

He sits next to her.

Odd, that rhymes. Um . . . Zamir. Um. Were you born here? What nationality are you? Have you ever held a regular job?

ZAMIR I'll tell you some other time. Tell me, are you in your father's will? Does his money go to you, or to your mother first? Is it shared between your mother and you?

FELICITY Why do you want to know?

ZAMIR I want to make sure he hasn't, you know, left his money to a butterfly or something. I'm lookin' out for you. A lot of wealthy people leave their money to pets and plants and appliances.

FELICITY Yeah. Well, I don't know about the will. I'm sure it goes to Mother, and then to me. And nobody leaves money to an appliance. That's a silly accusation.

ZAMIR Don't call me silly. I'll knock you into the middle of next week. I'll tie you to the bed and cover you with honey and release killer bees in the room. I'll burn all your clothes, and buy you three burkas to wear—one black, one black, and the third one black. And I'll black your eyes to match them.

FELICITY (*very taken aback*) Um. Uh . . . uh . . . .

ZAMIR I'm sorry, I told you I have a bad temper. And I hate those burka things, I'd never make you wear them.

FELICITY Zamir, are you sure you want to be married to me?

ZAMIR Yeah. I think you're cool. I want your parents to support us. I think they will eventually.

FELICITY Um . . . you don't feel that maybe we got married without . . . enough forethought?

ZAMIR Well, you were drunk, but that's not my fault. I was drunk too, but even when I'm drunk, I can still think straight. I'm one of those people who can drink and drink and it just makes me more charming.

FELICITY I see.

ZAMIR I hope you're not thinking about that bad word beginning with "a."

FELICITY Bad word beginning with "a"?

ZAMIR Annulment. I warn you not to look into that.

FELICITY Warn me? Like threatening me with killer bees?

ZAMIR No, this is America, I know that. You can't force American women to obey you. They're very independent and pig-headed and impossible to deal with. I should've married someone from my own country. Ireland.

Zamir pours two glasses of Fresca here He also puts some small pill in her glass; she doesn't notice.

So, rather than threaten you, I . . . "ask" you not to look into annulment. There's too much divorce in America anyway. It's bad for the children.

FELICITY (*thinks; there's no reasoning with him, she covers her thoughts*) Yes, I see your point. You have old-fashioned morality, I guess.

ZAMIR Yes, I do. You look very sexy tonight.

FELICITY I'm really rather tired.

ZAMIR Ooooh, sexiness and being tired. That's hot.

FELICITY Uh-huh.

ZAMIR You haven't had any of the Fresca I poured for you.

FELICITY Oh yes, thank you.

She sips it; he sips his.

ZAMIR I always loved Fresca. I think it's better than 7UP or Sierra Mist or Teem or Wink or Sprite or Squirt.

FELICITY Yes, it is.

She takes a second sip, gets very sleepy, her body goes limp; she's out like a light.

ZAMIR Oooooh, baby. Sexy.

Zamir starts to move his hands all over her unconscious body. He finds this exciting.

VOICE (*speaking after Zamir begins doing this*) He starts to move his hands all over her body. The audience groans uncomfortably. She remains asleep.

SCENE 5

The parents' house again. Felicity visiting her mother. The mother wears the exact same dress as in Scene 2, but in a different color. The dress is a shade of yellow.

FELICITY That's a nice color, Mother.

LUELLA Thank you, dear.

FELICITY Is that the same dress you were wearing yesterday, but just a different color?

LUELLA Yes, I like the dress. I think it flatters me.

FELICITY It is nice on you. Did you dye the dress since yesterday?

LUELLA No, dear, I bought ten of these dresses, all in different colors. To match my moods.

FELICITY How is your mood today?

LUELLA Kind of yellow.

FELICITY Uh-huh. Mother, I need to talk to you seriously. I have a problem and I don't know how to solve it.

LUELLA How is the city, darling? Are you still enjoying the culture, the nightlife, the museums, the theater?

FELICITY Not really.

LUELLA What about going to the theater? Remember your grandmother and I used to take you to Broadway musicals. You always loved them.

FELICITY Yeah. But I don't go to the theater much anymore. It's too expensive.

LUELLA Is it?

FELICITY Well, it's a hundred dollars a ticket.

LUELLA The shows must be very good then. What have you seen?

FELICITY I've seen 100 plays by Martin McDonough, I've seen 200 plays by David Hare, and 300 plays each by Tom Stoppard and Alan Ayckbourn and Michael Frayn.

LUELLA Are Americans not writing plays anymore?

FELICITY I don't think they are.

LUELLA Just as well. Americans are very stupid. And the British speak so well, of course. Although I did have one friend who killed herself during Brian Friel's *Faith Healer.*

FELICTY Really? Did she will her heart to stop beating?

LUELLA No, she took a gun out and shot herself in the head. Apparently Ralph Fiennes was very offended. (*pronounced Rafe Fines*)

FELICITY Well, I don't want to talk about theater anymore, I have more pressing matters to discuss.

LUELLA Who's your favorite British playwright?

FELICITY Um. I don't know. William Shakespeare and Molière.

LUELLA Oh yes, I've heard they're very good. Although I hear that Shakespeare didn't really write his plays, and someone else did. So I guess that *other* person is Shakespeare. Some earl.

FELICITY Uh-huh. You know, I'm reminded this is why I left home, we can't get the conversation to move forward in a linear way. (*firm*) Now listen to me: I have made a disastrous mistake. My husband is insane, and he's probably dangerous as well, and I need help getting out of the marriage.

LUELLA You know. Sometimes you have to give things time. I'm still giving things time with your father, and any day now I expect him to be different.

FELICITY Well, that's very sweet of you, or maybe just stupid, but Daddy at least doesn't try to kill you. He doesn't drug you and do God knows what to you at night.

LUELLA You know, darling, I don't like to discuss what happens at night. That's private, and it's unspeakable.

FELICITY It's unspeakable?

LUELLA No, I just mean, it's private. One shouldn't talk about it. I don't even talk about it to myself.

FELICITY Do you and Father . . . still have physical relations?

LUELLA I really don't know. If I kept a diary, I could check it. But I don't keep one.

FELICITY Gosh, maybe you're not the right person to help me. I don't quite know where to go for help.

Enter Leonard, the father, carrying a tennis racket.

LEONARD Did I hear my Princess needs help? Do you need help, Princess?

FELICITY Why do you call me Princess? You've never called me Princess before.

LEONARD I was just watching *Father Knows Best* on the TVLAND channel. Robert Young called his daughter "Princess." And then his son "Bud." "Hey, bud." Then his other daughter Kitten. Princess, Bud, Kitten. Here, kitty, kitty. That was a good time, the 1950s. Father knew best, Mother agreed with him, the children had their problems but they followed his advice, and things worked out. Of course, that was before "the gays" started living together and ruined heterosexual marriage.

FELICITY Speaking of ruined heterosexual marriage, Father . . .

LEONARD Were we?

LUELLA Are you playing tennis today, dear?

LEONARD What? Tennis?

LUELLA You're holding a tennis racket.

LEONARD Oh, is that what this is? I don't know where I got this. "Tennis anyone?" That's a famous line. What's it from?

LUELLA I think Enid Bagnold used it in *The Chalk Garden*.

LEONARD Enid who?

LUELLA Bagnold.

LEONARD The "what" garden?

LUELLA Chalk.

LEONARD Chalk. Like writing on the blackboard chalk? I can't understand anything you're saying.

LUELLA You're just not up on theater, darling.

LEONARD Well, I'm a man, you know. I like football. And butterflies. I hate theater.

FELICITY Oh, this visit is hopeless. I need help but clearly this is the wrong place to come.

LEONARD You need help, Princess? Kitten? What's the problem? Do you want me to have your husband killed?

FELICITY It's immoral to kill people.

LEONARD Is it? Even when you have a good reason, it's immoral?

FELICITY I want to get an annulment. I don't want Zamir killed. We can't just go killing people.

LEONARD (*disdainful*) Not kill people. I suppose you would've just stood there and let Hitler take over the world. You would've been like Neville Chamberlain and appeased Hitler. You would have said, go ahead, march your soldiers into the Rhineland, ignore the treaty of Versailles, see if I care!

LUELLA Your father is such a history buff. It's the only thing about him I love.

Felicity and Leonard stare at her.

LUELLA (*embarrassed, corrects herself*) It's ONE of the things about him I love. One of . . . several.

LEONARD Thank you, Luella. Soon we'll get those "colored lights going again," eh?

LUELLA (*uncomfortable with his seeming flirtation*) What?

LEONARD I wonder what nickname Robert Young had for his wife Margaret in *Father Knows Best*?

LUELLA He called her Margaret. So . . . that was her nickname.

LEONARD Perhaps I'll call you Margaret.

LUELLA Just don't call me late for dinner.

LEONARD What?

LUELLA (*despairing for a moment*) I need rest. I need to find a crevice in the rock of the world to hide in. No I don't. I'm exaggerating. I'm afraid the choice of yellow was too bright for me today. I need a softer color. Would you excuse me? (*exits*)

FELICITY Do you do terrible things to Mother at night?

LEONARD I don't know what you mean by terrible things.

FELICITY I don't know either.

LEONARD I'm thinking of writing you out of my will, to punish you for getting married when you were drunk.

FELICITY I think I was given a date rape drug. And I think I was given one last night too.

LEONARD Ah. Well, at least the young man has some spunk!

FELICITY What???

LEONARD Sorry. I sometimes identify with bullies, I don't know why that is. Let me have a different response. He gave you a date rape drug! That's horrific. I am appalled. How can I help you?

FELICITY Well . . . I mean, when something like this happens, isn't getting a marriage annulled easy? Or at least possible? But I can't let Zamir know I'm looking into it, he gets angry quickly and I . . . worry for my safety actually.

LEONARD Well, Princess, Kitten, Bud . . . you've come to the right person. I will investigate how we can get this man out of your life.

FELICITY By annulment. Not by hiring a hit man, right?

LEONARD Don't you worry, Princess. I'll take care of it.

FELICITY Legally though. Okay.

LEONARD I'm always legal. I'm over 18.

FELICITY Uh-huh. Can I see your butterfly collection?

LEONARD Why?

FELICITY I just want to see it.

LEONARD No. You might have germs, you might infect them.

FELICITY But they're dead.

LEONARD Still they can get skin diseases—impetigo, eczema, psoriasis.

FELICITY All right, forget it. I think I've got to go find a lawyer to help me get an annulment.

LEONARD I'll get you a lawyer. I have friends in the legal profession. Some of them owe me favors.

FELICITY No, maybe I better get my own lawyer.

LEONARD Princess, Kitten. Father knows best. Do what I say, I'm the father, I'm the man, and I know whereof I speak.

FELICITY And whereof do you speak exactly?

LEONARD Whereof? I'm protecting you. Let Daddy take care of it. You go home and have a nice nap.

FELICITY I don't want to go home. Zamir might be there.

LEONARD Well, go to a bar and get drunk then, I don't care. I have a phone call to make. Just don't do anything, and know Daddy will protect you.

FELICITY All right. Thank you, I think. (*starts to go*) But I want to see your butterfly collection someday, all right?

LEONARD Yeah, yeah.

Felicity exits.

Leonard makes sure she's gone. Starts to dial his cell phone.

Luella comes back in, wearing the same dress in a different color. This time green. He abruptly shuts his cell phone.

LUELLA I think I'm going to feel more comfortable in green today.

LEONARD Shut up. Go to your room, I need to make a call.

LUELLA Why are you using your cell phone in the house?

LEONARD I don't like that color. Go change your dress. Go make breakfast. Clean the house.

LUELLA You don't like the green?

LEONARD No, it's a putrid green. Go put on a . . . grape dress or something.

LUELLA I don't have grape. I have purple.

LEONARD Grape or purple, I don't care what you call it. Just go away and get out of that green thing.

Luella exits, upset and discombobulated.

LEONARD (*speed dials cell phone, speaks once person picks up*) Scooby-Doo? It's 3:10 to Yuma calling. I have something interesting to tell you. I think I may have come across a big one. I think he may be an operative. He may have lots of information that could save our country from another attack. Meet me at longitude 64 and latitude red code alert. Red code alert. (*annoyed, the person on the other line isn't understanding him*) Well, didn't you write these terms down? Look it up, and call me back if you can't figure it out. So let's meet at 1600 hours. 1600 hours. (*More annoyed, the person still is confused*.) All right, all right. 4 P.M. Meet me at 4 P.M. No, that's the wrong longitude. Look: meet me in the Butterfly Room at 4 P.M. Use the secret passageway. Is that clear enough for you? (*hangs up, annoyed*)

SCENE 6

A cocktail lounge. Felicity is sipping a cocktail, seated at a banquette-type table. She's depressed, worried. She finishes it.

VOICE (*on sound system*) May I get you another cosmopolitan?

FELICITY What?

She looks around, confused, doesn't know where the voice is.

VOICE (*on sound system*) Would you like another cosmopolitan?

FELICITY Uh . . . uh . . .

Enter the VOICE, *dressed in normal clothes that could pass for being a waiter in a nonfancy restaurant. His age is late 20s to early 40s, average-looking to handsome, pleasant demeanor.*

VOICE (*to Felicity*) I asked if you'd like another cosmopolitan. (*to the audience, friendly*) I'm going to be the waiter in this scene.

FELICITY Oh, there you are. I didn't know where the voice was coming from.

VOICE I'm a ventriloquist. Sometimes I forget I'm not onstage.

FELICITY Oh, I see. Well, sure I'll have another drink. My father told me to go out and get drunk. And it's been an awful morning.

VOICE I'm sorry.

FELICITY Thank you.

VOICE I'll bring you that drink.

FELICITY Oh, and can you put "What Are You Doing the Rest of Your Life?" on the jukebox for me?

VOICE If we can get the rights, I will. (*exits*)

A moment later, the sad song "What Are You Doing the Rest of Your Life" plays. Felicity sings along.

Note to anyone putting on a production: you must get the rights to Michel Legrand's "What Are You Doing the Rest of Your Life?" if you choose to use that melancholy song. You can also look at lists of songs in the public domain, and choose a "sad, I feel sorry for myself" song.

The music stops abruptly. Felicity stops singing along and looks surprised. The Voice comes back.

VOICE I'm sorry, those are all the rights we could get.

FELICITY (*a bit baffled*) Oh, I see.

The Voice exits.

A man comes into the restaurant. He's dressed casually, maybe wears a hat and/or sunglasses. He stops and notices Felicity. If he has sunglasses, he takes them off once he starts talking.

MAN Hello there! What a surprise seeing you here.

FELICITY I'm sorry?

MAN It's Reverend Mike. (*takes off sunglasses and hat*) I married you and Zamir the other night. I make porno on the side. Or maybe I make porno, and marry people on the side. It depends on the week which the major endeavor is. It's good to see you.

REVEREND MIKE *is between 32 and 45. He has a likable but slightly debauched face and aura. Kind of sexy too, but also unusual, a bit weird. A bit like a Mickey Rourke or a Kevin Spacey persona.*

FELICITY Oh! Hello.

REV. MIKE May I sit down? (*sits*)

FELICITY Yes, please. So you're Reverend Mike. I don't recognize you. I seem to have had a prolonged blackout the night I got married. Did I seem conscious during the ceremony?

REV. MIKE You were nodding off a bit. I thought maybe you were a heroin addict.

FELICITY I think Zamir put something in my drink.

REV. MIKE I'm glad you're not a heroin addict, that's good news. I used to sell heroin, but I think that was a bad thing I did, drugs aren't good for you. Selling them doesn't fit the Beatitudes, and I am a minister. It doesn't say, "Blessed are the dope pushers," does it? (*laughs*)

I think making porno is a better thing to do for people than selling heroin, because God created sex and it's holy and good and hot and fun, and people can't seem to stop watching it, so somebody's gotta film it. My next project is called *The Big Bang,* and it's going to have 27 orgasms.

And you know, it helps people out—they get some money for doing something fun, and though of course a lot of the performers are on drugs, I don't sell them the drugs, so it's not really my fault. But as it says in the Beatitudes, "different strokes for different folks."

FELICITY Tell me, how well do you know Zamir?

REV. MIKE I just met him the other night when I met you. He seems like a great guy. I'm meeting him here in a minute or two.

FELICITY You are?

REV. MIKE Yeah, he's having some trouble with his parole officer, and I said maybe I could put him on the Rev. Mike Porno Movie payroll so it looked like he had a job.

FELICITY He has a parole officer?

REV. MIKE Oh, I'm sorry, you didn't know that? Oh, shit. Oh well. I'm not the most discreet person in the world. Yeah, well don't tell 'im I told you, okay?

FELICITY Oh God, how am I going to get out of this?

Enter the Voice/Waiter with her cosmopolitan.

VOICE Here's your second cosmopolitan, even though it's two in the afternoon. (*looks at Rev Mike*) I didn't realize the scene was going to be crowded.

REV. MIKE Could I have a beer in a green bottle? No, I think a brown bottle would be better.

VOICE A brown bottle. Yes, sir.

REV. MIKE Hey. You look familiar. Were you in my film last week? Were you in the orgy scene in the dumpster?

VOICE No. I've never been in a film. I think you're confusing me with someone else. I'm a waiter and a ventriloquist.

REV. MIKE Oh, sorry. I don't always recognize people. I once sat next to Jane Fonda at *The Vagina Monologues* and I didn't recognize her. I just thought she was this hot-looking older woman.

VOICE I'll bring you a beer in a brown bottle. (*exits*)

FELICITY Did you like *The Vagina Monologues*?

REV. MIKE I did. I identified with them.

FELICITY Did Jane Fonda like them?

REV. MIKE I don't know. I like her mouth. I like your mouth. Hope Zamir is likin' it.

FELICITY No, I'm not happy with Zamir. When I talk about annulment he gets angry. He thinks my parents are going to support him.

REV. MIKE Maybe he needs a job. He could sell drugs. Weed's not that bad for you. Or maybe he could help me make porno.

FELICITY I don't understand in what way you're a minister.

REV. MIKE I'm a good person. I counsel people. I counsel married people too. Maybe I could counsel you and Zamir.

FELICITY But I don't want to be married to him.

REV. MIKE How come?

FELICITY Well, I don't know him. And I am angry he drugged me in order to marry me.

REV. MIKE Have you considered forgiveness?

FELICITY Forgiveness? Are you kidding?

REV. MIKE Jesus talked about forgiveness.

FELICITY Well, sure but . . . . I mean maybe in a few YEARS I could forgive him, but right now I'm pretty far from it.

REV. MIKE I don't think Jesus means for us to wait a few years. Forgiveness is a more transformational event.

FELICITY Sure, okay, but . . . look, what's your experience with *annulment*? Can you help me? Would you testify I was nodding off?

VOICE Zamir will probably be here in a minute and a half.

FELICITY Oh. Did you hear that?

REV. MIKE Hear what?

FELICITY I think that ventriloquist waiter said Zamir is going to be here in a minute.

REV. MIKE Really? I didn't hear anything.

FELICITY Oh. I must be hearing voices now, it's very upsetting. Look, don't tell Zamir you saw me, okay? I don't know why, just don't tell him. And if I want to reach you, how can I find you?

REV. MIKE You have e-mail? My screen name is MisterFloppy at earthlink.net No, that's wrong. HardMisterFloppy at earthlink.net. I used to be PartyDickMisterFloppy at earthlink.net, but then I got clean.

FELICITY Okay. My e-mail is Felicity at msn.com.

VOICE (*offstage, over sound system*) Felicity leaves the restaurant.

FELICITY Oh, I think I better leave the restaurant.

VOICE (*sound system*) You probably don't want Zamir to see you here.

FELICITY (*to Voice*) No, you're right. (*to Reverend Mike*) It was good, sort of, to meet you, Reverend Mike. I may contact you about testifying.

She starts to exit.

VOICE (*sound system*) Too late. Zamir arrives, and Felicity is still here.

Felicity crouches down in booth, to hide.

Enter Zamir. He stops when he sees Felicity and Reverend Mike.

ZAMIR What's this?

REV. MIKE Hey, Zamir. Been talkin' to your foxy lady. She's awesome.

ZAMIR How did you get in touch with each other? (*to Felicity*) What are you up to with him?

FELICITY Nothing. We met by chance. I didn't even know what he looked like. He said hello to me.

REV. MIKE Yeah, it's true, bro. I was comin' in here to meet you, and pow—I just saw her and thought, hey that's that chick who married Zamir and was so wasted.

ZAMIR (*to Felicity*) I thought you were going to your parents to talk me up.

FELICITY Well, I did that . . . but then I got thirsty.

ZAMIR So you aren't here plotting against me, right?

FELICITY No, Zamir. Why would I do that?

ZAMIR I can't imagine. But then American women are insane. But I can tame them. I can tame you. (*sits down with them; to Mike*) She's lookin' sexy today. Don't you think so, Mike?

REV. MIKE Yeah. I was tellin' her I liked her mouth before you got here.

ZAMIR I don't want you talkin' to her about her mouth. Her mouth belongs to me now.

FELICITY My mouth doesn't . . .

ZAMIR What?

FELICITY Nothing. Forget it. It's hopeless.

ZAMIR Hey, good news. I found your credit cards.

FELICITY You did?

ZAMIR Yeah, the police found your purse and I showed them our marriage license, and they left it with me.

FELICITY Oh that's good. That's great the credit cards were there.

ZAMIR Yeah, but you know, your credit cards are all maxed out.

FELICITY What? You . . . tried to use my credit cards?

ZAMIR I was trying to buy you a present. Jeesh, give me some credit here, I was doing a nice thing. But I didn't know I'd married a debtor.

FELICITY I'm not a debtor. I just got behind in some stuff. And you can't just use my credit cards.

ZAMIR I'm your husband. What's yours is mine, and what's mine is yours except I don't have anything.

FELCITY Give me back my credit cards right now. And did the police really find them? Or did you take them the night of the so-called wedding?

ZAMIR What?? What did you say?

REV. MIKE Hey, hey, calm down, people. Think of Jesus and the marriage feast at Cana. He turned water in wine. Let's have some wine.

FELICITY I already have a cosmopolitan.

REV. MIKE Well, then let's all sing Hymn number 33.

FELICITY What's Hymn number 33?

REV. MIKE "Puff the Magic Dragon."

FELICITY That's not a hymn.

REV. MIKE Yes, it is.

ZAMIR Hey, wife-y over there. I'm not through talkin' to you. First of all, the police returned your stolen bag. And if you hadn't gotten so drunk, we could have run from that mugger, but you could barely walk, let alone run. Second of all, don't go accusing me of pretending we got mugged. If I say something, it's true. Even if it's false, it's true, you got that?

FELICITY That doesn't make sense.

ZAMIR I'm the husband. Shut up. And third of all . . . I used your credit cards to buy you a present. I wanted to make you happy. And fourth of all, you keep hurting my feelings.

FELICITY You married me when I was unconscious!

ZAMIR I'm used to arranged marriages. In Ireland.

REV. MIKE Hey. You two need to chill. You both need a time-out. Wowie, zowie. You folks need some spiritual solace. Have you ever tried forgiveness? Have you ever tried peyote? I don't sell it anymore, but we could ask around.

FELICITY Why don't you stick to pornography?

REV. MIKE Don't talk about it like it's a bad thing. God created sex. And He watches it, why shouldn't we?

FELICITY You know, I have to go . . . (*can't think what to say*) . . . see my mother about . . . a horse.

ZAMIR A horse?

FELICITY Yeah I . . . am going to take riding lessons. May I have my credit cards back?

ZAMIR I left them in our apartment.

FELICITY Okay. Well, I'll see you later, Zamir. Nice to meet you, Reverend Mike. Next time don't marry someone who's nodding off.

REV. MIKE Sorry, but I don't want to discriminate against heroin addicts. I know a lot of them. They're sweet but troubled.

FELICITY Never mind.

Felicity exits.

REV. MKE Gee, I'm a bit worried about your marriage, bro.

ZAMIR I'm an optimist. Her father is going to give her and me money, or else maybe he'll die and leave her his money. And she'll learn to adore me. Everybody does. Except my fuckin' parole officer.

REV. MIKE Hey. We'll work that out, bro.

ZAMIR Really? Good. Let's get drunk first, okay? I'm feelin' stressed.

REV. MIKE Bacchus, the god of wine.

ZAMIR Not wine, beer. (*calls out*) Two beers.

VOICE (*responding from offstage via the sound system*) Two beers, coming up. And meanwhile, we wonder what Felicity's father is up to.

Zamir and Reverend Mike frown, not quite sure what they've heard.

Scene 7

Darkness at first. We hear the voice of HILDEGARDE.

HILDEGARDE (*in darkness*) Hello? Hello?

LEONARD (*in darkness*) Scooby-Doo? Is that you?

HILDEGARDE What?

LEONARD It's 3:10 to Yuma. Permission to enter.

HILDEGARDE What?

LEONARD Push the door.

HILDEGARDE Hello? I'm here.

LEONARD Push the door!

HILDEGARDE Push it. It won't move. Oh yes, it will. I think I'm in.

LEONARD Yes, I think so.

HILDEGARDE Hello, 3:10 to Yuma. Scooby-Doo is here, reporting for duty.

LEONARD Wait. Let me clap the lights on. (*He claps.*)

Lights up. We are in the "Butterfly Room," but there are no butterflies. Instead there are many, many guns in a case and/or mounted on the wall. Maybe grenades scattered around too. Maybe big cans that say "gasoline" and "ethyl." We see Leonard and Hildegarde.

Hildegarde is a pleasant-faced, conservatively dressed woman of 40 to 50. A nice, neat hairdo. Maybe a navy blue skirt, a navy blue jacket, a white blouse, and pearls.

LEONARD Thanks for getting here so fast.

HILDEGARDE I used the secret entrance so your wife wouldn't see me.

LEONARD She's watching some theater thing on *Great Performances* now anyway.

HILDEGARDE (*referring to the guns, gleefully tongue-in-cheek*) I like your butterfly collection. Very pretty.

LEONARD Yes, it is pretty, isn't it? (*points to an assault rifle*) This is my new Solomon Island Birdwing. Do you like it?

HILDEGARDE Oh, very much. (*friendly, changing the topic*) I brought you a little card. Because we haven't seen each other in a while.

Hildegarde hands him a card.

LEONARD Another card, huh? You and these cards.

HILDEGARDE It's a way of saying hello.

LEONARD Right, hello. (*opens the card*)

HILDEGARDE Do you like the picture?

LEONARD A little girl holding her heart in her hand and offering it to a little boy. Although her chest isn't bleeding, how can she be holding the heart?

HILDEGARDE It's not a violent card. It's a friendship card.

LEONARD I like the violent cards better.

HILDEGARDE They're hard to find. (*encouraging him*) Read what I wrote inside.

LEONARD (*reads*) I am so glad I know you. You are the best! With admiration and affection, Hildegarde.

HILDEGARDE Do you like the sentiment? Because that's how I feel! You are the best. The United States is lucky to have you as part of its shadow government. And in time maybe the coup will finally be completed.

LEONARD Sssssh. Don't say that kind of thing out loud. What if the room was bugged?

HILDEGARDE Oh, I didn't think of that. (*speaks loudly*) "I am a Democrat! I hate all these conservative judges."

During the previous lines, Hildegarde's panties fall down around her ankles, but she doesn't seem to notice. Leonard does notice, but isn't sure how to bring it to her attention.

LEONARD Well, never mind, I don't think I'm bugged. (*He looks back down at her panties around her ankles.*) Hildegarde. Are you feeling a draft?

HILDEGARDE What? (*smiles, enamored of him*)

LEONARD I think your panties are showing.

HILDEGARDE Oh my goodness, are they? (*She looks down at her ankles, genuinely surprised.*) Oh my goodness, I'm so embarrassed. The elastic in the waist has been loosening, I'm so sorry.

Hildegarde reaches down and pulls her panties back up under her dress. She has no self-consciousness doing this.

HILDEGARDE There! Hope they stay up for a while.

LEONARD For a while? Has this been happening all day?

HILDEGARDE Yes, but don't let it bother you. Just something about how the Chinese are making the elastic in panties these days, it just seems to stretch too far in like 6 minutes.

LEONARD I see. Well, I called you because I need your help. I think my daughter has married a terrorist, and I have a hunch—but my hunches are good as you know . . .

HILDEGARDE I do know. I think your hunches are very good.

Her underwear falls down again around now.

LEONARD And my hunch says he knows something about the terrorists' plans . . . (*looks down at her underwear*) Hildegarde, your panties have fallen down again.

HILDEGARDE Oh dear, I'm so sorry. I feel so embarrassed. But you know the elastic is just totally gone. Maybe I should just leave them there, and forget it.

LEONARD Well, if you're going to leave them there, why don't you just take them off entirely?

HILDEGARDE Well, I don't feel comfortable not wearing underwear.

LEONARD But you're not *wearing* it. They're down about your ankles like some insane shoe accessory.

HILDEGARDE Well, don't get angry. I'm not doing it on purpose. Just ignore it. (*pulls up her underwear*) You should be looking at my face anyway. (*smiles*) I'm looking at your face. I take strength from it.

LEONARD (*not that interested on her crush on him*) Well, that's nice, Hildegarde, thank you. But we need to focus on business. Do you have your little tape recorder with you?

HILDEGARDE It's inside my bra.

LEONARD (*frowns*) And is your bra FIRMLY attached to your body?

HILDEGARDE Oh, yes. It's very secure.

LEONARD That's good.

HILDEGARDE Very good. It's very secure. Oh, I have greetings from Tiny Tim and Tuptim.

LEONARD Oh, that's nice. I don't remember who they are.

HILDEGARDE They're in the State Department. The cripple and the effeminate Asian man.

LEONARD Oh, yes. Right, they've helped us out, haven't they? Well, say 3:10 from Yuma says hello back.

HILDEGARDE Roger that.

LEONARD (*sighs*) This isn't a game, you know, Hildegarde. This is deadly serious. And the future of our country and the entire world depends on the work that I and the others in the (*whispers*) shadow government (*regular voice*) are doing.

HILDEGARDE You're right, Leonard. I know. I'm sorry I said "Roger that."

LEONARD That's all right. Now I need you to trail my son-in-law, Zamir the terrorist.

HILDEGARDE Oh, we definitely know he's a terrorist?

LEONARD Yes, we do. I feel as certain about it as if he had been pointed out to us by some warlord we paid money to.

HILDEGARDE Oh. That's quite certain then.

LEONARD But I feel we need the final proof he's a terrorist before we kidnap him and use "enhanced interrogation methods" to get the secrets out of him so we can protect our country.

HILDEGARDE Oh. Final proof. Yes. I can see that would be helpful.

LEONARD (*looks at her like she's stupid, but goes on*) I contacted Looney Tunes and got him to shadow Zamir, and he's followed him to a nearby restaurant. But I can't use Looney Tunes inside the restaurant because of his inability to stop making Road Runner sounds . . .

HILDEGARDE Oh, is that what he's always doing. I thought it had to do with Nascar.

LEONARD No, it's Road Runner. It's a kind of Tourette's but connected to cartoons. That's why he's called Looney Tunes.

HILDEGARDE Oh, I love our code names. I don't like Scooby-Doo that much. Can I have another one? Like Ethel Barrymore?

LEONARD I don't want to call you Ethel Barrymore. Let's discuss this at another time. I need you to get to this restaurant . . . (*hands her piece of paper*) . . . and without drawing attention to yourself, tape Zamir's conversation and see if we can get anything on tape that would justify our torturing him.

HILDEGARDE Oh, are we going back to it's okay to torture?

LEONARD No, no, of course not. We'll stick to John Yoo's torture definition very closely.

HILDEGARDE I've forgotten what that is.

LEONARD How could you forget such a significant thing? John Yoo from the Justice Department wrote a torture memo that says it isn't torture unless it causes organ failure. And even if it does that, as long as the president says the words "war on terror," it's A-okay.

HILDEGARDE Oh, that's right. He's such a brilliant lawyer, John Yoo, and how I love the Federalist Society.

LEONARD But you're wasting time in fond recollection of Justice Department triumphs. We can't begin to interrogate Zamir in an enhanced manner until we get a bit more information. So you must get to that restaurant and record his conversation.

HILDEGARDE Copy that, roger. Oh, I'm sorry. I mean, yes, darling, I'll be glad to. I don't mean "darling," I mean Roger. (*Her underwear falls down again; she doesn't notice.*) I'm sorry, I mean Leonard. (*laughs*) I'm off! (*starts to exit*) I'm very off! (*laughs*) Sometimes all this cloak-and-dagger stuff makes me giddy. It's so different than when I was a debutante in San Antonio all those many moons ago.

LEONARD Hildegarde, stop. If you keep walking with your underwear that way, you're going to fall down.

HILDEGARDE Oh sorry. I'll keep pulling it up. (*She pulls them up; kind of holds them in place by clutching them through her dress around the waist.*)

LEONARD Do you want me to get you a pair of my wife's panties?

HILDEGARDE No. I don't feel that would be proper.

LEONARD Do you want to wear any of my underwear?

HILDEGARDE (*tempted*) *Oh . . .*

LEONARD I mostly wear jock straps. Do you want to wear a jock strap of mine.

HILDEGARDE Oh, you know, I don't think that sounds feminine at all. I think I'll just stick with my ladies' garment and just hold on to them better.

LEONARD I could get you duct tape.

HILDEGARDE No, no. Let me go do your bidding, and see what I can find.

LEONARD All right, thanks, Hildegarde.

HILDEGARDE You're welcome. And you may get another card from me soon.

She exits. He frowns. Picks up a gun. Kisses it.

LEONARD Oh, my beautiful butterfly. (*kisses it*) How I wish there was a group of 200 to 300 people in front of me . . . (*He aims the gun at the audience.*) And I could use my Second Amendment right to form a militia, and I could mow the entire group down.

VOICE Looking outward, Leonard considers killing the audience.

LEONARD (*holds the gun on the audience*) But, of course, I'm alone in my Butterfly Room, and there's no one to kill. (*lowers the gun, puts it down*) But there may be other killing ahead, for the cause of Freedom. Operation New Jersey Freedom.

Scene 8

Back at the restaurant. Zamir is there with Reverend Mike. There are two empty beer bottles on the table.

ZAMIR I don't understand this whole "you gotta have a job" stuff. I mean, I'm not meant to work. I'm an entrepreneur. I'm a venture capitalist. I make deals. I can't go work at Walmart or something.

REV. MIKE Well, that's why I should put you on the payroll.

VOICE (*enters*) Here are two more beers, even though you've already had four and you haven't had any food and it doesn't look like you're going to order any.

ZAMIR Can you not talk so much when you bring the beers?

VOICE Sorry, sir. I'll try. Here are your two beers. Although you've already had four. But who's counting? (*exits*)

ZAMIR You know, I don't like that. I don't like the way he just spoke to me. He . . . what's the phrase . . . he dissed me, man, right? Hey, four eyes! Hey, waiter boy!

Zamir goes toward where the Voice/Waiter exited. He looks violent. Reverend Mike follows him to stop him. The waiter does not wear glasses, by the way. It's just miscellaneous name calling that popped into Zamir's brain.

While they move toward stage right, Hildegarde peeks over the banquette, looking at them. Or she enters here, not seen by them, and hides.

Note: if your set doesn't allow for Hildegarde to hide behind the banquette, come up with some other obvious solution such as her hiding behind a door, or underneath another table, etc. She's not a very good spy.

REV. MIKE Zamir, Zamir! Cool it, man.

ZAMIR He dissed me, he dissed me. Fuck that shit, man.

They head back to the table. Hildegarde quickly ducks down behind the banquette.

REV. MIKE Zamir, look, don't go assaulting someone, okay? You wanna end up back in the pokey?

ZAMIR The pokey? What pokey?

REV. MIKE The slammer, man. *Oz*. That TV show, not the munchkins, you know the HBO prison show. Real intense, man. You don't want go back there.

ZAMIR Yeah, but he treated me like I was dirt.

Hildegarde aims her tape recorder and/or its microphone in Zamir and Reverend Mike's direction. It's very obvious to the audience. The two guys don't notice.

REV. MIKE Hey, Zamir. Blessed are the peacemakers, man. Remember that, that Jesus said. Now let's talk about porn, man.

ZAMIR Don't talk all that Christianity stuff, Mike.

REV. MIKE Okay, let's talk porn. I'm a porn again Christian. And look, I can put you on the books and it can look like you're working. Plus, I was thinking, you're a good-looking guy . . . why don't you join the fun? You know, in front of the camera?

ZAMIR Really? I don't know. It sort of goes against my upbringing.

REV. MIKE God created lust, man. It's part of the whole thing. Look, next Tuesday, we're doin' it—*The Big Bang,* that's what we're callin' it. And they're goin' be doing it all over, man—in New York, in D.C., in San Francisco. And you can be part of it. Shoot it out, man. I mean, explosions, man, all over the place. It's gonna be awesome. Dirty, dirty. The Big Bang.

ZAMIR Can I wear a mask?

REV. MIKE Sure.

Suddenly there's a very distinct cell phone ringtone behind the banquette. Very melodic. Goes on a long time. They look surprised, look around a second. Hildegarde creeps out from her hiding place, trying to act as if hiding is normal.

HILDEGARDE I'm so sorry. I forgot to turn my cell phone off. Would you excuse me?

She starts to run but trips because her underwear is around her ankles. They run up to her. She sprays mace in their faces. They scream.

HILDEGARDE Sorry, sorry! I can't stay. Bye! (*runs off, escapes*) Oh, my God! Oh, my God!

Lights start to dim. We hear some or all of the following as the lights are dimming:

ZAMIR My eyes. My eyes.

REV. MIKE We got maced, bro.

ZAMIR Who was that?

REV. MIKE Some nutty lady, I don't know.

SCENE 9

Leonard and Luella's house. The kitchen nook again. Leonard, Luella, and Felicity are sitting close together.

FELICITY I'm feeling in crisis. Why haven't you been able to find me a lawyer yet?

LEONARD I'm still looking. Be patient, Kitten.

FELICITY Well, I don't feel safe. And he's staying in my apartment now. He's calling it "our" apartment.

LEONARD I'm working on it. Don't rush me.

LUELLA Darling, are you still enjoying the nightlife? The excitement, the museums, the theater? What have you seen lately?

FELICITY Stop talking about theater, would you? I hate theater.

LUELLA Darling, it's life you should hate, not theater. No, I don't think I mean that. Theater is based on life, isn't it? I remember *Mary, Mary* by Jean Kerr. She was married to the critic of the *New York Times,* Walter Kerr. Then I think she went mad and was institutionalized. No, I think I'm thinking of Charles Lamb's sister Mary. Jean Kerr was fine. She had a cocktail. Do you like this color dress?

Leonard's cell phone rings.

Onstage left in a spot is Hildegarde, her panties around her ankles. She is on her cell phone.

LEONARD Let me take this. It may be about the lawyer.

He speaks into his cell phone, standing a bit apart from his family.

Hello. Leonard Mugatti here.

HILDEGARDE 310 to Yuma? It's Scooby-Doo. (*She reaches down and takes her underwear off, to free her ankles; back into the phone*) I just took my underwear off.

LEONARD What is the nature of this phone call, please?

HILDEGARDE Sorry, I'm just so thrown. I had to spray them both with Mace. Thank goodness I had some with me.

LEONARD What happened, please?

HILDEGARDE Leonard, darling, I don't mean darling, I mean, commander, commander and fellow worker in the shadow government, I think you are one hundred percent right and I got it on tape, but I kept falling and that's why I took my underwear off.

LEONARD Get to the point.

HILDEGARDE Listen to what I wrote down. "Next Tuesday, we're doin' it next Tuesday. The Big Bang, that's what we're callin' it. And they're goin' be doing it all over—in New York, in D.C., in San Francisco. And you can be part of it." He said that to Zamir. And then he said: "Explosions, man, all over the place. It's gonna be awesome. Dirty, dirty." Maybe that means dirty bomb. Or maybe worse. And then he said it again: The Big Bang.

Enter Zamir. He's rubbing his eyes, look frazzled.

ZAMIR (*to Felicity*) There you are. I couldn't find you. I need some eyewash.

Zamir exits.

LEONARD (*into phone*) I must hang up now. Something has happened here. Meet me where we met earlier today. Longitude, latitude, right? As soon as you can. Do you copy that?

HILDEGARDE Copy, roger that. See you soon, darling. I don't mean darling. Or maybe I do. Oh, Leonard, we're going to stop an attack, aren't we?

LEONARD I think so, Scooby-Doo. I do think so. Good-bye.

He hangs up; Hildegarde exits her spotlight, leaves.

LUELLA Scooby-Doo? Who's Scooby-Doo, Leonard?

LEONARD Scooby-Doo is a talking dog from an animated series. It is also the name of a first-class litigator that I had been calling for my daughter.

Zamir enters.

FELICITY Oh. I see.

LEONARD Now, Zamir. What were you saying a moment ago?

Leonard stares at Zamir. Felicity and Luella stare at both men.

ACT II

Scene 1

Same setting as before, the kitchen nook. Felicity and Luella are there. Luella is talking, moving her mouth convincingly, but it's as if the sound is off. Her mouth keeps moving. Felicity looks worried, keeps looking around and out, distracted.

After a while, the Voice speaks. He stands in a spot on the side of the stage, apart from the two women. He addresses the audience directly in a friendly, "narrator-like" tone. He wears a dark suit probably.

VOICE Felicity's mother continued to talk about theater, and which plays and musicals she had seen. She talked about *Wicked* again. She said she identified with Elphaba, the green girl who was unpopular in witch school. She talked about *Les Miz*, or *The Miserables* as she called it. She said she liked stories about the French Revolution, and thought it was stirring to put the aristocrats in their place, but she didn't like it when they cut their heads off. On the other hand, there wasn't any beheading in *The Miserables*, and Felicity's mother liked that.

She liked the revival of *A Chorus Line*. She felt if she had taken another life choice, she might have been a dancer, and could have been someone like Cassie, briefly a star, and then faced with the more limited option of just trying to get into the chorus line and sing a song called "One" behind some celebrity or other. Who was that celebrity, Felicity's mother wondered, the One who was sung about? Was it Lauren Bacall? Was it Angela Lansbury? Was it Mrs. Patrick Campbell, the mistress of George Bernard Shaw?

Sometimes Felicity's mother's mind free-associated and free-associated until she was in some alternative reality where she didn't have to think about anything.

LUELLA (*we hear her voice suddenly*) And who was the celebrity they were singing about in the song "One"? Was it Lauren Bacall? Was it Angela Lansbury? Was it Mrs. Patrick Campbell? Of course that's a silly thought, she's from 1893, and the song "One" takes place in 1976 or so, I think, right? So it wouldn't be someone like that. Maybe it was Ann Miller. She was in *Sugar Babies* around then, and she had that great hairdo and those tappy-tappy toe abilities. I loved Ann Miller. She seemed like a nut, but a really nice nut.

Luella's mouth continues moving, and no sound comes out again.

VOICE But Felicity just couldn't listen to her mother chattering on anymore. She was worried about her father. And though she didn't really like him, she was worried about Zamir. Her father had taken Zamir up to the second floor to get eyewash for him; he refused to let Felicity and her mother do it.

And now they hadn't been seen or heard from for almost two hours. She asked her mother if that seemed normal, but her mother said she didn't know what normal felt like, and then just kept talking about theater. And Felicity kept thinking, where was her father, and where was Zamir? And why did Felicity have a scared feeling in the pit of her stomach?

The spot on the Voice goes off; he exits.

LUELLA You know I don't really know what normal is. That's one of the reasons I go to the theater. To learn that.

FELICITY Mother, if you keep talking about theater, I'm going to have to hit you.

LUELLA Is it normal for a daughter to threaten her mother with hitting? I don't know the answer. That's my dilemma. Perhaps if you actually hit me, I could evaluate it better.

FELICITY I'm sorry, Mother, I don't want to hit you. I just want you to stop talking about theater.

LUELLA Oh, you don't want to hit me. That's makes me so happy. Thank you, dear.

FELICITY Mother, I'm really worried. Where are Father and Zamir? They haven't been back for almost two hours.

LUELLA I can't imagine where they are. I wonder if they fell asleep. Or maybe he's showing him his butterfly collection.

FELICITY I don't believe he has a butterfly collection. I think the room is used for something else.

LUELLA You don't think it's connected to all that "shadow government," do you?

FELICITY Shadow government? What do you mean?

LUELLA Nothing, dear. Pretend I said nothing. Do you remember that play *Pack of Lies* about the next-door neighbor who was a spy for the communists. That talented Dana Ivey played the part of the spy. And Rosemary Harris played my part.

FELICITY I'm starting to want to call the police.

LUELLA Oh, I wouldn't do that. The police really like your father, he goes to all their spaghetti suppers, and he donates money to them.

FELICITY Well, surely they'd help if someone's being held against their will, wouldn't they?

LUELLA Well, I'm a little afraid of them. Remember those Halloween children your father thought were Mexican immigrants attacking us? Luckily he didn't kill them, just some superficial wounds on their arms and legs. But one of the parents tried to press charges against your father, and the police arrested them and kept them overnight, and then the next day, the parents suddenly withdrew the charges. So I'm a little dubious about criticizing your father to the police. I don't think they like it.

FELICITY Goodness, I never heard about that.

LUELLA Yes, the family moved away. Probably back to Mexico. Oh, that's right, they weren't Mexican, so it couldn't be "back" to Mexico. Actually, I don't know where they went. Maybe into the witness protection program.

FELICITY I'm going up to the so-called Butterfly Room. This isn't normal just to sit here and do nothing.

LUELLA Normal. It's such a conundrum for me.

SCENE 2

The so-called Butterfly Room. With all the guns. Leonard and Hildegarde are there. Hildegarde is holding her underwear in place, her hand pressed against her dress.

Zamir is tied to a chair, in his underwear. He also has one of those "ball contraptions" in his mouth used in S/M (a rubber ball in his mouth, somehow tied around his head).

A new person is there too (Looney Tunes, played by the Voice). He wears a trench coat and maybe a fedora. He has very high energy. Looney Tunes speaks like various cartoon characters—Elmer Fudd, Road Runner, Foghorn Leghorn, Daffy Duck, Sylvester, etc.

LEONARD This is taking too long. It took an hour to get his clothes off and put that ball in his mouth.

HILDEGARDE I'm sorry, Leonard, it's exciting, but I'm just a little . . . unprepared for it all.

LOONEY TUNES Beep, beep! (*makes a car driving sound, then a screeching stop sound:*) Urrrrrrrrrrrrrrrrrr . . . eeeeeeeeecccchhh! Beep, beep!

LEONARD Did you have something to say?

LOONEY TUNES Beep, beep!

HILDEGARDE Oh, it's nice to see Mr. Looney Tunes again, and now I understand what he's saying. I used to think he was just making noises.

LEONARD He is just making noises.

HILDEGARDE Yes, but it's connected to his nickname. Hello, I'm Scooby-Doo, remember me? I'm also a cartoon, but I want a different name.

LOONEY TUNES Scooby-Doo. Dooby Scew. Yucka-wucka.

LEONARD Don't say so much in front of the terrorist. We don't want them to know what our secrets are.

LOONEY TUNES Beep beep. I have thuggestion. I tawt I taw a puddy tat!

LEONARD In what way is that a suggestion?

LOONEY TUNES I say, I say, I say boy, let's do Chinese Water Torture boy. That way he'll talk! Beep beep, urrrrrrrrrrrr . . . .. eeeeeeccchh!

LEONARD No, we don't have time for that drip drip drip stuff. We need something faster! Now the next step . . .

HILDEGARDE Roger darling, I mean Leonard sir . . .

LEONARD Don't interrupt me. The next step is to decide how to interrogate him and what enhanced techniques to apply, and in what order. My plan is to . . .

HILDEGARDE But why do we have to do anything? I thought we were going to send him off to Syria and let them make him talk? I feel a little squeamish about . . . you know, doing "enhanced" things to him.

LEONARD Have you forgotten 9/11?

HILDEGARDE No, I remember it. Why do you ask?

LEONARD That's why we do all this. They attacked us on 9/11. We are protecting ourselves and our country. If we don't fight them over there, we'll have to fight over here.

HILDEGARDE Yes, but he's over here already, so my point is, why can't we send him to Syria and let them deal with it?

LOONEY TUNES Beep, beep! I say, I say, Chinese water torture!

LEONARD Hildegarde, we don't have the time for rendition. (*whispers*) There's an impending attack.

HILDEGARDE Oh, so it's a time issue. Yes, of course. Silly me. I guess we . . . have to face up to what we must do. Oh, dear.

LEONARD What's the matter now?

HILDEGARDE I'm afraid I faint easily.

Outside the door, Felicity knocks on the door.

FELICITY Father, what are you doing in there?

Zamir starts making sounds, but they're indistinct due to the ball in his mouth. Hildegarde is nervous.

LEONARD Felicity, go away. I'm busy in here.

FELICITY Where is Zamir?

LOONEY TUNES (*sounds of driving, sounds of brakes applied*) Urrrrrrrr, eeeeeeeecccch! Beep, beep! Wacky wabbit!

FELICITY What's going on in there?

LOONEY TUNES Beep, beep!

LEONARD We're watching cartoons. We're bonding. Leave us alone.

LOONEY TUNES Beep, beep! Uuuuuur.

Leonard signals they should all make sounds like cartoons.

LOONEY TUNES Des*th*picable! Sufferin' succotash!

LEONARD What's up, Doc?

LOONEY TUNES Be vewwwy quiet; I'm hunting wabbits.

Leonard signals Hildegarde to make a cartoon sound.

HILDEGARDE Ummm . . . Auntie Em, Auntie Em! There's a tornado!

Leonard looks mad and waves at Hildegarde to be quiet.

LOONEY TUNES Pepe le Pew—p.u.! Eeeeer, beep beep!

Leonard waves his arm impatiently, telling everyone to be quiet.

LEONARD I've turned the sound off now, Felicity. I want you to go away.

FELICITY I want to see Zamir. I want to see if he's all right.

LEONARD He's fine. He has a ball in his mouth.

FELICITY What?

LEONARD Nothing. Leave us alone.

FELICITY Father, this is not normal behavior.

LEONARD These are not normal times, daughter.

FELICITY I'm going to go get help. But I will be back. Father, I do not want you to hurt Zamir.

LEONARD I'm working on the annulment, Princess. Zamir is open to it.

FELICITY Zamir, if you're in there, I'm going to find help. I don't know what, but I'll be back. (*leaves*)

LEONARD Damn it, we have to move faster. We've got to make him talk. Let's start by breaking his fingers.

HILDEGARDE Wait. We haven't even asked him a question yet.

LEONARD You have to do something violent first, or they won't respect you.

LOONEY TUNES Beep beep, bweak duh fingah!

HILDEGARDE No, please. We have to at least ask him to tell us about the impending attack. And then if he refuses, you can threaten him, and ask him again. And then if he refuses a second time . . . well, I guess I could leave the room, and you two could do . . . whatever you think best to protect the country and all of us.

LEONARD Just ask him the question. That seems ridiculous. He'll just lie.

HILDEGARDE Well, please, let's START by asking him, all right?

Leonard starts to take the ball out of his mouth.

Where did you ever get this ball contraption, Leonard? It's so peculiar.

LEONARD It was a gift for my wife once, but she didn't like it.

He stops taking the ball out to focus on Hildegarde.

HILDEGARDE Really? A gift for your wife? How would she ever use it?

LEONARD Hildegarde, you're oddly innocent. Someone should nominate you for the Supreme Court. Although we may do away with the courts. But if we keep them, you should be made a member.

HILDEGARDE Oh, what a sweet thing to say. And I've done so little in my life to justify it. But I'm always glad to do what little I can to help my country. And to help you, Roger, I mean Leonard. I'm sorry my brain has a glitch that keeps coming up Roger.

LEONARD Let me finish this. (*to Zamir*) Do not scream when I take this out, or I will immediately break your nose.

Leonard takes the ball out of Zamir's mouth. Zamir looks scared but angry. He doesn't scream.

LEONARD I hope you realize the seriousness of your position.

LOONEY TUNES Beep beep. (*to Zamir, with quiet but threatening intensity*) Wacky wabbit. Owivia deHaviwwand.

LEONARD (*to Voice*) Be quiet.

ZAMIR May I have a glass of water?

LOONEY TUNES I say, I say Chinese water torture, boy!

LEONARD Stop saying that!

HILDEGARDE I'll get him some water.

LEONARD No, no water. (*to Zamir*) We're giving you a chance to save yourself. What is the Big Bang and when is it supposed to happen?

ZAMIR What?

LEONARD Hildegarde heard your conversation in the restaurant. The Big Bang, explosions, New York, L.A., D.C. When and how?

ZAMIR *The Big Bang* is a porno movie. You've misunderstood. It's a porno movie. Explosions means orgasms, not bombs.

LEONARD So much for asking for the truth. Now we move on to torture.

Leonard starts to put the ball back in his mouth. Zamir screams. Hildegarde looks worried. Voice is happy.

LOONEY TUNES Urrrrrr, errrr. Beep, beep! Wodents and wabbits! Intewwogating tewwowists! (*As the lights dim to black, he keeps speaking excitedly.*) Sewere fewocity! *Ex*-skew-ciating suffewing in duh cause of duh war on tewwah!

Scene 3

Felicity and her mother downstairs in the living room. Felicity is looking at the phone, nervous.

FELICITY Mother, I'm really worried. I hope he looks at his e-mails frequently and that he calls me. Luckily I remembered his screen name, HardMisterFloppy at earthlink dot net. I hope it was earthlink. (*to herself*) Was it?

LUELLA What did you just say? I didn't follow it.

FELICITY I want that reverend who married me and Zamir to come help us. I'm afraid to call the police if Father pays them.

LUELLA Did you ever see that Sidney Kingsley play called *The Detective Story* set in a police station? What was it called, I wonder?

FELICITY You just said it was called *The Detective Story*.

LUELLA They made a movie of it, and it was Lee Grant's first big break. And Eleanor Parker played Kirk Douglas's wife, and she'd had an abortion that Kirk Douglas didn't know about. It was very intense.

Phone rings. Felicity answers it.

FELICITY Hello? Oh good, is this Reverend Mike?

LUELLA I think Lee Grant won an Oscar for it. Or did she win an Oscar for *Shampoo*?

FELICITY I'm so glad you have such memorable screen names.

LUELLA In a different life choice, I could've had Lee Grant's life, and never met your father, and won an Oscar.

FELICITY I need help from someone. I think my father is holding Zamir captive.

LUELLA Eleanor Parker and that abortion, it created such a fuss. Lots of screaming and crying. She probably got nominated too, I think. Your father is pro-life, did you know that?

FELICITY Mother, I'm on the phone. (*into phone*) We can't call the police for . . . complicated reasons . . . so I'm hoping maybe you could come over here and help.

LUELLA Leonard is so forceful, but he says he's "pro" life. Very sentimental about early life fetuses. Or would they be called fee-ti?

FELICITY (*gently to her mother*) Sssssssh. (*into phone*) Well, I don't know what's going on, it's just Zamir showed up and my father took him upstairs, and then they disappeared. Two hours ago.

LUELLA And then he loves all those stem cell things.

FELICITY And I knocked on the door but he said Zamir had a ball in his mouth.

LUELLA They're smaller than a pinprick from a tiny needle, did you know that? But your father just loves those stem cells. Wants to give them the right to vote, just about.

FELICITY Do you have a way to get here? Do you have a car?

LUELLA Wants to register them as Republicans, I guess.

FELICITY Oh, a motorcycle's even better, probably. We're in Maplewood. Can you MapQuest it?

LUELLA Can you MapQuest it? That's something our grandmothers never said. They used maps then. Or bread crumbs.

FELICITY Yes, New Jersey.

LUELLA I said to your father, why do you want to give stem cells the vote, that's complicated, why don't you just steal the election like you did in Ohio in 2004?

FELICITY Mother, dear, can you hold your thoughts for a while? (*back into phone*) It's 37 Edgeware Drive. I don't know the zip.

LUELLA Oh, and Terri Schiavo. He was obsessed with that woman.

FELICITY Mother, do you know the zip code here?

LUELLA No, dear, ask your father. I can't be bothered with zip codes. Your father says we're all going to be tattooed with bar codes, and rounded up and shot if we write letters to the editor.

FELICITY (*into phone*) Reverend . . . oh, all right, Mike . . . I can't get the zip code, just put in Maplewood and get here as fast as you can, okay?

LUELLA Do you remember that poor Schiavo woman? On the news every night, her mouth open, her brain dead. Your father had this intense connection to her. Why don't you marry her? I said. Don't think I wouldn't like to, he said. Oh, he's weird.

FELICITY (*into phone*) Am I in love with Zamir? Hardly. I mean he drugged me and he was trying to use my credit cards, but . . . well, I don't think he should be harmed though,

LUELLA He'd point at her on the television and scream, "Life is precious!" And he wanted her hooked up to tubes and breathing contraptions for ever and ever.

FELICITY Look, we can't keep talking. Do the MapQuest, hop on your motorcycle, and come help, okay? I don't know what's going on up there.

LUELLA I mean I'm functional and can breathe and eat on my own, and I don't find life "precious." (*as if she heard Leonard say something*) Shut up! (*back to her train of thought*) I find it terrifying.

FELICITY Okay, bye!

Felicity hangs up, takes in her mother, who seems to be peaking.

LUELLA I mean, if I jump out the window and then fall into a coma, I don't want your fucking father connecting me up to machines and tubes and respirators and keeping me alive for years and years like I'm some sort of PET ROCK. Pull the plug, damn it, pull the plug! (*She weeps.*)

FELICITY Mother, what's the matter? I missed how you got here. What happened?

Felicity rocks her mother in comfort; Luella's weeping starts to subside.

LUELLA (*vulnerable, a bit lost*) I'm sorry, darling, I was just remembering *The Detective Story* by Sidney Kingsley.

Scene 4

The Butterfly Room. Zamir's T-shirt now has a few blood spots on it, as if they did small cuts on his chest and arms. The ball is in his mouth. Leonard and Looney Tunes (Voice) are there. Hildegarde is hovering a bit away from it all. Her underpants are maybe around her ankles again.

LEONARD Hey, scumbag. You ready to tell the truth?

Zamir makes unhappy noises with the ball in his mouth.

HILDEGARDE Oh, don't hit him again.

LEONARD Stop interfering.

HILDEGARDE But he can't answer with that thing in his mouth. It's like when the dentist asks you questions when you have all those things stuck in your mouth. It's really not fair.

LEONARD Shut up. (*to Zamir*) Hey, scumbag!

Leonard hits Zamir, who screams.

HILDEGARDE (*about to faint*) Ohhhhh. (*faints*)

LEONARD Oh, for God's sake. Hildegarde, I find your behavior offensive.

LOONEY TUNES She's so squeamish! Beep, beep! Ware Wabbit! Wuff wider at duh wodeo!

LEONARD Looney Tunes, I know you can't control that, but control it, would you?

LOONEY TUNES Fuck you! Weece's Peanut Butter Cup!

Hildegarde sits up, a bit disoriented, looks around.

LEONARD Hey, Hildegarde, stop passing out. Pay attention.

HILDEGARDE I'm sorry, Leonard. I just always envisioned we'd have time to send him out for rendition. To Syria, or Egypt. I'm finding having it in front of me is just too vivid.

LEONARD (*to Zamir*) You ready to have the ball taken out again? (*takes it out*)

ZAMIR Oh, God, help me.

LEONARD You want some more homemade acupuncture on your chest?

HILDEGARDE Leonard, maybe I could go home. Or bake cookies for everyone.

LEONARD Don't say my name!

HILDEGARD I'm sorry. I just . . .

LEONARD Hey, Zamir. (*screams*) WHEN IS THE ATTACK GOING TO HAPPEN? WHAT COUNTRY IS BEHIND IT?

ZAMIR THERE ISN'T GOING TO BE AN ATTACK! IT'S A PORNO MOVIE. IT'S A FUCKING FUCK FILM, YOU FUCK FACE!

Leonard punches Zamir very hard; Zamir falls over backward and passes out. Hildegarde starts to faint again, but doesn't. Voice/Looney Tunes runs in circles, delighted.

LOONEY TUNES Viowence, viowence! Scwutinze the viowence! Wabbit wun!

ZAMIR Don't hit me, don't hit me.

LEONARD Tell me the truth then. When is the attack?

ZAMIR There is no attack.

HILDEGARDE Let me talk to him. (*to Zamir*) Please, Mr. Zamir, I'm saying this for your own good. Please tell him, or he may kill you. John Yoo says he can do anything that doesn't cause organ failure, and that gives him an awful lot of leeway.

LEONARD Don't talk to him about John Yoo. You're getting ridiculous, woman.

ZAMIR It's a porno film.

HILDEGARDE Stop telling him that.

ZAMIR It's the truth.

HILDEGARDE I don't care. Tell him something else, or it's going to be very bad for you.

LEONARD Scooby-Doo, mind your business! (*Picking up small garden clippers or scissors, he grabs Zamir's hand and isolates a finger.*) I'm going to cut off one of his fingers.

HILDEGARDE Please, Mr. Zamir, say something.

ZAMIR The attack is scheduled for tomorrow at noon.

LOONEY TUNES (*softer, interested*) Beep, beep.

LEONARD What else?

ZAMIR There will be three attacks. New York, L.A., and Chicago.

LEONARD Scooby-Doo's notes said you said D.C.

ZAMIR I meant D.C.

LEONARD Suicide bombers or missiles?

ZAMIR Missiles.

LEONARD (*to Hildegarde*) And you say "enhanced techniques" don't work. If you had your way, we'd be attacked tomorrow.

Looney Tunes/Voice steps forward, takes off his hat, and addresses the audience in his regular voice. The others onstage freeze. Lights dim to black on the scene; a spotlight illuminates the Voice in his Narrator role.

VOICE You could cut the tension with a knife, or with a machete. Leonard looked at Hildegarde with hatred. He knew he was going to report her to the shadow government. She was a disappointment, even though she had been the one who gathered the terribly important information about the attacks tomorrow at noon. Leonard wondered if it was wise to hurt Zamir some more physically before asking what country or countries were behind the missile attacks. It probably was. But as soon as he got the answer, he would make a red alert call to Crouching Tiger in the Pentagon, so that a preemptive strike could be initiated against those countries. This was one of those moments the shadow government had been preparing for. (*said in a normal way*) Beep beep. Meanwhile, in the living room, Reverend Mike has arrived. He hasn't gone upstairs yet, though, because Felicity's mother won't stop talking.

SCENE 5

Felicity and Luella downstairs. Reverend Mike is now there. He is sitting next to Luella, feeling a little trapped, but being polite, while she talks. Felicity may be standing, anxious to take Reverend Mike away from her mother and up to whatever's going on upstairs.

LUELLA It's just because you're a minister, I thought you might know the play, and might appreciate its message.

FELICITY Mother, he said he doesn't know it.

REV. MIKE Sorry, Mrs. Mugatti, I don't go to the theater that much. You know, when you're marrying people and makin' porno, you're just kind of busy.

LUELLA *The Madwoman of Chaillot* was Jean Giraudoux's attempt, some say, to make the citizens of France feel better after World War II when they learned the extent to which some of their fellow citizens had collaborated with the Nazi invasion.

FELICITY Mother, I want him to come upstairs with me.

LUELLA In a minute, dear. The Countess Aurelia was a bit touched in the head, like me, some would say. Would you say I was touched in the head, Felicity?

FELICITY Yes, Mother, I would. Now may we go upstairs?

Felicity tries to get Reverend Mike off the couch, but Luella grabs his arm.

LUELLA Wait a moment. The Countess Aurelia saw that there were industrialists and oil magnates and businessmen who were going to ruin Paris, her dear Paris, and she said, "No, this cannot happen." She also said, and I sometimes say this to myself when I'm weeping, "Nothing is ever so wrong in this world that a sensible woman can't set it right in the course of an afternoon." Only I'm afraid that's not true anymore, do you think, Reverend Mike?

REV. MIKE I really don't know.

FELICITY Come on, we have to go upstairs.

Terrible offstage screams. Zamir screams in agony. Leonard and Hildegarde can be heard yelling offstage as well.

LEONARD (*from offstage*) Come back here, you bitch!

HILDEGARDE (*screaming from offstage*) Help, help!

FELICITY Good God, what's that?

Hildegarde comes running in. She has some blood on her dress, presumably from Zamir.

HILDEGARDE Help, help! There isn't much time. We have to call the White House and stop those missiles from being launched!

LUELLA More company, I wish someone would've warned me.

FELICITY Who are you?

HILDEGARDE Who am I? (*takes the question very seriously*) I don't know if I can take the time to answer. I'm a loyal Republican, I love my country, I have a crush on someone who I think is your father and (*to Luella*) your husband, I'm very sorry. I've never been married, and I get these crushes on certain powerful men . . .

FELICITY No, forget it. Where's Zamir?

HILDEGARDE He told your father about the attack, and he called Crouching Tiger at the Pentagon, and I think they have ordered immediate missile strikes against Iran, Jordan, and Uzbekistan. So we have to act fast.

LUELLA This sounds like *Dr. Strangelove*. Does anyone remember that film?

HILDEGARDE I told your father I think he has it wrong. Mr. Zamir kept saying "The Big Bang" was the title of a pornographic film, but your father kept hurting him until finally he said it was code for attacks on our country tomorrow at noon.

REV. MIKE *The Big Bang* IS the name of a porno film. Zamir was right.

HILDEGARDE Oh. It's my fault, I misunderstood, it was an understandable mistake. (*sudden panic*) Where are my panties??? (*remembers*) Oh, that's right, he put them on Zamir's head, something about sexual humiliation and Muslims, and now because of what I thought I heard, now there will be many deaths, and maybe world war. Oh God.

Enter Leonard, with two small plastic grocery bags. He has some blood on him.

LEONARD What have you been telling them? Don't believe a word she says—she's a turncoat and a traitor to the United States of America!

HILDEGARDE Oh, Leonard!

FELICITY Why are you both covered in blood?

LEONARD Have you forgotten 9/11?

HILDEGARDE Leonard, we have to contact Crouching Tiger. This man was the one I saw in the booth with Mr. Zamir, and he says "The Big Bang" *is* the name of a pornographic film.

REV. MIKE I'm supposed to start filming tomorrow. Zamir was going to be in it, albeit in a mask. But if there are going to be missiles coming at us, maybe we should postpone the filming.

LEONARD No, we'll be able to stop the missiles coming at us. Crouching Tiger will attack the three countries Zamir finally told us about.

FELICITY Where is Zamir? Is he all right?

LEONARD It was hard to get him to tell me which countries were bombing tomorrow. (*hands her the two bags*) Here are three of his fingers, and here is his ear.

Felicity looks in the "fingers" bag and faints. Hildegarde faints. Luella faints. Leonard and Rev. Mike stare at each other.

LEONARD Who are you?

REV. MIKE Wow, his fingers and his ear. Gosh, that's hard for a man of God to take in.

LEONARD The Islamic terrorist threat is the gravest threat the civilized world has ever faced. These people are NUTS. And if I have to cut off fingers and ears to keep my country from being attacked, then I'm proud of it.

REV. MIKE Huh. It's the name of a porno film, dude. It's not a scheduled attack. If you can stop those preemptive bombs aimed at those three countries, I think you should call up that . . . Crouching Tiger person . . . and do that. Whaddya think? Can you do that, pal?

LEONARD You're a friend of the terrorist. I can't trust you either. I think I'll let the preemptive attack play itself out. Even if the information ends up being wrong, still it's good foreign policy to bomb those particular countries.

REV. MIKE Huh. Wow. Sometimes different strokes for different folks can go too far.

Enter the Voice, no longer dressed as Looney Tunes. He is in a spot. The women remain fainted on the floor, and Leonard and Reverend Mike continue to stare at each other.

VOICE The women had fainted dead away, and they had not yet recovered. They didn't really wish to return to consciousness. They preferred to be in the realm of Hypnos, the god of sleep. Leonard and Reverend Mike stared at one another. They couldn't figure out what topics of interest they had in common, and so conversation seemed difficult, and they remained mostly silent, though Reverend Mike continued to say "wow" from time to time.

REV. MIKE Wow.

VOICE After a bit, Felicity came to.

Felicity sits up, looks around.

She had been unconscious for a few minutes, which is long for fainting. She looked around and didn't know where she was for a moment.

FELICITY Oh, my. Where am I? Did I faint? Something is really bothering me. What is it?

VOICE Then it came back to her—her father bloody, the strange woman named Hildegarde also bloody, and distressed. The gruesome grocery bags containing fingers that once belonged to Zamir, and an ear as well, and which had been taken from him in exchange for a lie that might cause a world war.

FELICITY Oh, dear. No, no, I don't . . .

VOICE Felicity did not like her present reality.

FELICITY Oh . . . I don't like this. I don't like what's happened. There's no way I can imagine a positive outcome from this. I don't want to be part of it.

VOICE Felicity wished to disengage from reality, or disengage from this play, or perhaps both. Which did you mean, Felicity?

FELICITY I don't know, I think both. Umm . . . can we go back to an earlier time in the play, and have . . . I don't know . . . different things happen.

Luella and Hildegarde have been starting to come to also.

HILDEGARDE Yes, I vote for different things happening too.

LUELLA Me, too. This is all very disturbing, and I'd love to go back and redo some of it.

FELICITY First of all, I want to go back to before Zamir had his fingers and ear cut off. I don't find that acceptable, and it upsets me as a dramatic event.

LEONARD What the fuck is she talking about? These liberals refuse to face reality. If we don't stand up to the Islamic terrorists, we will all be killed and our civilization will perish.

FELICITY He's not a terrorist, Father. You tortured someone because you misunderstood plans for making a pornographic film.

LEONARD Making such a film is a bad thing. There's no morality in this country.

FELICITY Father, I think I would like to force-feed you these fingers and this ear. Can anyone help me tie him up?

LUELLA Yes, dear, let me get some rope.

LEONARD I'm willing to die for my country.

FELICITY Wait, I'm sorry. I can't do violence against him, that's ridiculous, that's escalating, I want to get out of this section of the play, I want to redo it. I just don't know how to fix Father. He seems very far gone. He needs empathy lessons. Father, can you feel any empathy for the man whose fingers you just cut off?

LEONARD I was doing it for a higher purpose.

FELICITY I want you to feel his pain.

LEONARD I don't feel it. He's a terrorist. And if he isn't, well, he shouldn't have acted like one, so everything that happened to him is his fault.

FELICITY Oh, God. I can't fix him. Can you feel empathy, Father? Ever? I want you to think of a fetus . . . in the womb, very young. The mother slips on a rug and falls on her stomach. And the fetus inside feels pain.

LEONARD It feels pain. Poor fetus. Poor, poor fetus. (*feels moved*)

FELICITY Well, that's lovely. It would be nice if you could have empathy for people living outside the womb. But I suppose this is a start.

LEONARD Poor little guy.

FELICITY (*hands him the two grocery bags*) I want you to take these bags from me and go back upstairs and reattach the fingers and the ear.

LEONARD I'm not a surgeon.

FELICITY Nonetheless, that is what I want you to do. Think positive thoughts, and I'm sure you can handle it. In the meantime, I intend to go back to an earlier section of the play so this story ends differently.

LEONARD I don't know what to do.

FELICITY Go upstairs and try, would you? Just try.

Leonard looks baffled, but exits with the two grocery bags.

Now let me see.

VOICE Felicity tried to think where in the past she wanted to go, and she realized it needed to be before her father became so suspicious of and hostile to Zamir.

FELICITY That's right. Let's go back to where I introduce my parents to Zamir.

HILDEGARDE Oh. I'm not in that. I'm going to go clean up and take a Xanax.

REV. MIKE I'm not in that either. I'll join you.

Exit Hildegarde and Reverend Mike.

LUELLA All right, dear. Let's try to do this.

FELICITY Yes, I agree.

Scene 6

Going back in time. The lights change in some strange and disorienting ways. There are loud sounds of machinery making intense grinding sounds, as if the attempt to move back to earlier in the play is an enormous effort. With a sort of abrupt sound of a screeching halt, suddenly we are back in Scene 2 of the play, where Felicity introduces her parents to Zamir for the first time.

Onstage are Felicity and Luella in the living room.

LUELLA Who did you marry, dear?

FELICITY Um . . . he's a . . . you know, I don't know what to say about him.

LUELLA What does he do for a living?

FELICITY You know, I asked him that too. And he refuses to say. (*signals for Luella to come closer, lowers her voice*) I don't want him to hear us.

LUELLA Who, dear?

FELICITY He's in the other room.

LUELLA Who is, dear?

FELICITY I have a funny feeling about him. I'm afraid he might be a terrorist. Or in the Mafia. Or bipolar. Or a serial killer. Or maybe just a drug addict and out of prison on parole.

LUELLA Who are you talking about, dear?

FELICITY My husband, my husband, my husband!

Enter Zamir. He is dressed as in Scene 2 of Act 1.

ZAMIR Hello, did you call?

Felicity quickly looks at his fingers and his ear, to make sure they're intact. They are.

FELICITY Oh good, you look fine! I'm very relieved.

She gives him a quick hug. A lot of relief.

Yes, Zamir, I did call. This is my mother.

LUELLA Felicity tells me she's afraid you're a terrorist. I hope she's mistaken. Is she?

ZAMIR (*to Luella*) Hello, Mrs. Ratzywatzy. I'm your new son-in-law, Zamir. It's so nice to meet you.

LUELLA Nice to meet you, Zamir. How did you and my daughter meet?

ZAMIR We met at Hooters.

LUELLA And who is Hooters?

FELICITY Okay, now Father comes in, I think. And you say, "Ooooh, oooh, do I smell French toast."

LUELLA I do? I don't remember that. Ooooh, ooooh, do I smell French toast?

Enter Leonard. He looks fine, and is not bloody.

LEONARD I incinerated a group of squirrels that was trying to get in and destroy my butterfly collection.

LUELLA Oh, I guess it wasn't French toast. What a shame. I love French toast.

ZAMIR Are you Felicity's father?

LEONARD Who are you?

ZAMIR I'm your daughter's husband.

LEONARD I didn't give my permission.

ZAMIR I didn't ask for it.

LEONARD I say you're not my daughter's husband.

ZAMIR I say you're not her father.

FELICITY Uh-oh . . . slow down. Don't get angry.

LEONARD I say you're robbing this house, and I killed you in self-defense. (*takes out a gun, aims it at Zamir*)

FELICITY Oh dear. Um . . .

ZAMIR (*takes out his cell phone*) And I say I will blow up the house with my cell phone.

FELICITY No, no, we agree on French toast. Let's talk about that!

LEONARD Don't push me, Mohammed, I will kill you!

ZAMIR My name is Zamir, you fuck face, and it's Irish!

FELICITY STOP! I was wrong. We have to go farther back than this. Things won't end any better if we start here. We have to go back . . . to our meeting at Hooters.

LEONARD What?

LUELLA (*as if it's an unknown and magical word*) Hooters.

Scene 7

The stage changes radically. Wonderful mirror lights spin and fill the stage with circling light. Lush romantic music plays, as in a 30s or 40s or 50s nightclub. We are now in a lovely nightclub/restaurant.

There should be a small bar on the side of the stage.

The Voice enters in a tuxedo. He is the maître d', and very elegant and charming.

VOICE Good evening, and welcome to Hooters. The home of elegant dining, dancing, floor shows, and great big breasts. And now two of our hostesses who may look like Luella and Hildegarde but they're not.

Enter Luella and Hildegarde. They look nice actually, except they have large breasts attached to the front of the costumes. They are not naked breasts, they match the dress material, but they are too large for their bodies. Maybe they wear cheap wigs, just so we know it's not them.

LUELLA & HILDEGARDE Welcome to Hooters.

LUELLA I'll be your server, Mary. And I have a 55 G cup size.

HILDEGARDE And my name is Sherry, and I have a 58 D cup size.

LUELLA Let's hope our cup sizes don't capsize.

They share the joke and laugh happily, and exit.

Enter Felicity, dressed nicely for an evening out. The Voice greets her as the maître d'.

VOICE Good evening, Madam, and welcome to Hooters. We are happy to welcome you to fine dining and dancing and a floor show. May I show you to a table?

FELICITY I think I'll just get a drink at the bar.

VOICE Certainly, Madam. Let me bring you to the bar.

FELICITY Okay.

It's a very short walk to the bar.

FELICITY (*to Voice*) Well, that was quite a journey.

VOICE My pleasure. Let me know if I can assist you in any way.

FELICITY Thank you.

Reverend Mike has slipped behind the bar. He is the bartender. He is not as elegantly dressed as the Voice. Still, he is dressed appropriately to be a bartender in a nice place.

REV. MIKE Good evening. Whaddya drinkin'?

FELICITY A vodka tonic, please.

REV. MIKE An excellent choice, for a Thank God It's Friday kind of evening, even though it's Tuesday.

FELICITY (*laughs*) Yes.

Enter Zamir. Dressed nicely if casually. He looks around, looking for the manager. He sees the Voice/Maître d'. He goes over to him.

ZAMIR Excuse me, I'm looking for the manager. I'm applying for the dishwasher position.

VOICE I'm sorry, the manager is not here this evening. He'll be in tomorrow at noon.

ZAMIR Oh. There's not anyone else in charge while he's gone?

VOICE Well, not for hiring, no. Come back tomorrow.

ZAMIR (*annoyed*) All right.

The Voice/Maître d' exits. Zamir looks around, just to take the place in. He's planning to leave, but he sees Felicity at the bar. He thinks she's attractive. He goes over to the bar, though not directly to her.

REV. MIKE (*bartender*) May I help you, sir?

ZAMIR Yes, a Rusty Nail please. Heavy on the rust.

REV. MIKE I'm not sure what that means, sir.

ZAMIR I don't know what it means either. Just sounded good. Make it strong, I guess.

REV. MIKE You got it. (*turns around to make the drink*)

ZAMIR (*to Felicity*) That's a pretty dress you're wearing.

FELICITY What? Oh, thank you.

ZAMIR Would you like another drink?

FELICITY I'm still working on this one.

ZAMIR We could have a second one waiting.

FELICITY Well, it's been a tough day at work. I think I'd like to get a little drunk.

ZAMIR (*flirtatious*) Sounds like a good plan.

REV. MIKE Here's your Rusty Nail, sir.

ZAMIR Thank you.

REV. MIKE Bottoms up.

ZAMIR And another for the lady.

REV. MIKE You got it.

Music starts to play underneath. The Voice/Maître d' and Hildegarde/Sherry dance in the middle of the mirror ball reflections.

FELICITY Oh, I didn't know they had dancing at Hooters. Really, it's much nicer here than I imagined.

ZAMIR Yes, the dancing is nice.

Felicity keeps watching the dancing. Zamir looks around, makes sure no one is looking at him, and surreptitiously puts a pill in her drink.

FELICITY (*turns sharply to him*) Did you just put something in my drink?

Music stops abruptly, the Voice/Maître d' and Hildegarde/Sherry stop dancing and watch the exchange between Felicity and Zamir.

ZAMIR No, I didn't.

FELICITY Yes, you did. I won't have that. We're doing it over so it's pleasant, and that's not pleasant.

ZAMIR I don't understand. You want us to have different characters?

FELICITY No, not different characters. I want us to have the same characters but . . . better ASPECTS of those characters.

ZAMIR Wow. Okay. Not quite sure but . . . I guess okay.

FELICITY And I shouldn't say I'm going to get drunk. It was probably the pill AND the alcohol that did me in. So I don't want that other drink.

ZAMIR (*to bartender*) Forget the refill for the lady. And take this one away, and bring her . . . just a seltzer.

REV. MIKE Okay. (*clears the drink, brings the cranberry one*)

FELICITY Good, now let's say all that didn't happen. Let's go back to "I didn't know they had dancing" and your saying, "Yes, the dancing is nice."

ZAMIR (*a little bothered but semi-willing*) All right.

Music resumes. Maître d' and Hildegarde/Sherry go back to dancing as if nothing has happened.

FELICITY I didn't know they had dancing at Hooters. It's a much nicer place than I knew.

ZAMIR Yes, the dancing is nice.

FELICITY Oh, look it's my parents.

Luella and Leonard dance into the space, and the Maître d' and Hildegarde/Sherry exit. Luella is herself now, and no longer has the strapped-on breasts she had before. She is wearing a version of her usual dress but it is fancier, more like what a woman might wear to a fancy place that has dancing. Leonard is dressed nicely, maybe in a suit or even a tuxedo.

Luella sees Felicity and leaves Leonard for a moment. He continues to dance with his arms outstretched as if she's still there. She goes over to Felicity.

FELICITY Mother, what are you doing here?

LUELLA I was telling your father about some play I had just seen, and he said, "Shut up," which I'm used to. But then to my surprise, he said, "Do you want to go dancing?" Because he forgot my birthday two months ago, but he just thought of it. And I thought that was pleasant of him to suggest dancing.

FELICITY That is pleasant of him.

LUELLA And while we were dancing, he stepped on my toe, and guess what? He said, "I'm sorry. I hope that didn't hurt too much."

FELICITY He did?

LUELLA Imagine. He wondered how I was feeling. I know it's a small hope, but if he thinks about my crushed toe, maybe we can build on that little bit of empathy? What do you think? Dare I eat a peach?

FELICITY Well, it is a glimmer of hope.

LUELLA And hope springs eternal, to coin a phrase.

Leonard stops dancing, suddenly realizes Luella isn't there.

LEONARD (*a bit annoyed, but not awful*) Luella, where the fuck are you?

LUELLA Oh, dear, I better go back. Sorry, darling, here I come.

Luella goes back to dancing with Leonard.

ZAMIR Weird to have your parents here at Hooters.

FELICITY Yes, I didn't know they'd be here. But my mother and I are trying to look for any glimmers of hope with my father.

ZAMIR Oh yeah? (*looks at his hand and his fingers*) Good luck.

FELICITY Now, now. None of that happened. And it's not going to happen. As long as we pay attention to what we're saying. Our present creates our future. So let's be careful. And hope springs eternal, to coin a phrase.

Enter Hildegarde, now herself again. She does not have the strap-on breasts. She has underwear around her ankles. She's wearing sunglasses. She seems focused on Leonard and Luella. She goes over to the bar.

REV. MIKE Excuse me, may I help you?.

HILDEGARDE (*to Rev. Mike*) Could I have a Shirley Temple please?

REV. MIKE A Shirley Temple? Wow, it's a long time since I've heard somebody order that.

HILDEGARDE Sssssh. Speak softer, I don't want anyone to know I'm here. (*She looks up or offstage, to be less noticeable.*)

FELICITY Look, it's that woman who tape-recorded you in the future. But that's not going to happen this time.

Hildegarde takes out a small pair of binoculars and looks at Leonard dancing with his wife. The Maître d' comes over to Hildegarde. Leonard and Luella may dance offstage in a little bit.

VOICE I'm sorry, Madam. We require patrons to wear underwear.

HILDEGARDE (*indignant*) I *am* wearing underwear. (*pause*) I wear them low.

VOICE I'm afraid they're causing comment among the hoi polloi.

HILDEGARDE Oh, for heaven's sake. (*she pulls her underwear up, unself-consciously*)

VOICE Thank you, Madam. (*walks away*)

HILDEGARDE Really, some things should be private, don't you think?

REV. MIKE I agree with you. To me a consenting adult should be able to wear their underwear any way they like.

HILDEGARDE Well, thank you!

REV. MIKE Tell me, would you like to dance?

HILDEGARDE Well . . . thank you very much, yes.

Reverend Mike and Hildegarde dance. She's holding her underwear up through her dress.

FELICITY Can you imagine someone having a crush on my father?

ZAMIR No, I find it very difficult to imagine.

FELICITY Okay, let's go back to redoing stuff. Um . . . . what do you do for a living, Zamir?

ZAMIR How do you know my name?

FELICITY I knew it from before. I'm sorry. Let me say it a different way. What is your name?

ZAMIR My name is Zamir.

FELICITY Oh. What an unusual name. My name is Felicity.

ZAMIR How felicitous.

FELICITY (*laughs, friendly*) Yes, very.

ZAMIR What do you do for a living?

FELICITY Oh. I'm an administrative assistant. I return phone calls, I make lunch reservations, I keep track of my boss's schedule. It's fine, I sometimes think I should go back to school and study philosophy. I'm sure there are lots of good jobs out there for people with a philosophy degree.

ZAMIR Really?

FELICITY No, that was a joke.

ZAMIR Oh, sorry. I wasn't sure. Didn't want to laugh at your dreams.

FELICITY Oh. What a lovely thing to say. Suddenly I like you.

ZAMIR Oh. You do. I started out liking you.

FELICITY What do you do for a living, Zamir?

ZAMIR What?

FELICITY What do you do for a living? Do you have a job?

ZAMIR Sure. I do stuff. Sometimes I drive a big van in the middle of the night, and I deliver things, and I get paid. Or I get a tip from someone where I can score something big. And sometimes I just find money . . . under a rock, you know.

FELICITY Under a rock?

ZAMIR Yeah, I do something for somebody, it's a little dangerous, maybe a little illegal; and they tell me to go to . . .

FELICITY No!

Music stops. Anyone dancing or onstage stops and watches Felicity and Zamir.

You see, that's part of the scary side of your personality. I don't like that. Now I'm remembering from the future, which we're not going to do the same way again . . . that you've been in jail and have a parole officer, so I'm assuming some of what you just said is probably true, right? Or are you making it all up to seem interesting or something?

ZAMIR God, you're so aggressive. Can't we just have a conversation?

FELICITY No, we can't. Now, do you actually get money from under rocks? And *why* do you have a parole officer? And is part of your parole that you have to get a job?

ZAMIR I'll tell you some other time.

FELICITY Fine, I'm going to go home. Which is just as well, if you don't get to know me, then you won't meet my father, and you'll be safer.

ZAMIR Just as well.

FELICITY Good-bye then. (*She starts to leave.*)

ZAMIR Wait.

She stops in her tracks. Everyone else stands still too.

I don't want you to go.

FELICITY Why?

ZAMIR I don't know. Let's keep talking. It's sort of a date, right? That's very American, a date, right?

FELICITY I suppose. But you have to talk more normally if I stay. (*She crosses back to him.*)

ZAMIR (*simple, truthful, no longer with swagger*) I only got money under a rock once. I delivered something for somebody. I don't even know what it was. And I have a parole officer because I got in trouble with credit card fraud.

FELICITY Well, that's not good to hear. But I appreciate your telling me.

ZAMIR And I came in here to apply for a dishwasher job. To keep my damn parole. And my parents are from Pakistan and they run one of those grocery stores 28 hours a day, 30 hours a day, and I used to work there with them when I was a teenager, and I thought I'd lose my mind. I want a more interesting life than that.

FELICITY I see.

ZAMIR There, now I'm as boring and stupid as dishwater, right?

FELICITY No. I can see why you would feel trapped at your parents' store. I probably would too.

ZAMIR I'm not sure that this is a different aspect of my character. This may be a different character.

FELICITY Well, even so, I prefer it. (*to the couples*) Okay, go back to dancing.

Music returns. Hildegarde and Reverend Mike go back to dancing. If you chose to have Leonard and Luella exit earlier, they return and continue dancing now. If they did not exit, they go back to dancing too. Hildegarde's underwear falls down as soon as she starts dancing again.

REV. MIKE You know . . . I wonder . . . may I offer to hold your underwear for you?

HILDEGARDE Oh, would you? How gallant.

She takes the underwear off. Reverend Mike puts his hand through it, "wears it" on his arm.

LUELLA Look at that crazy woman who just took her underwear off. And in a nice place like Hooters too.

LEONARD (*defensively*) I have no idea who she is. I've never seen her before.

LUELLA What? Well, who said you did?

FELICITY Strange Hildegarde is meeting Reverend Mike in this scenario. Maybe she'll get over my father. That would be healthier. Women need to make wiser choices for themselves.

ZAMIR Oh, I hate all that feminist stuff, makes me wanna puke.

Music stops abruptly. Couples stop dancing too, watch Zamir and Felicity.

She's dancing with a porno minister. You think that's some sort of wise choice? American women make me so . . . . (*He doesn't finish.*) I'm sorry.

FELICITY That hostility runs kind of deep, doesn't it?

ZAMIR My father is rather . . . strict. He had a big influence on me.

FELICITY I didn't take after my father.

ZAMIR Well, you're not the male child in the family.

FELICITY No, but I guess I'm saying you don't have to be your father. You can choose to be . . . your better self.

ZAMIR (*not hostile, but somewhat resistant*) You are full of . . . . ideas. I find I want to disagree with you and agree with you both at the same time.

FELICITY They say, it's a sign of intelligence to be able to hold two contradictory thoughts in your head at the same time.

ZAMIR Or is that schizophrenia?

FELICITY No, it's intelligence.

We now hear the Voice over the loudspeaker. I hope it's as if the Voice is taking her to the next beat . . .

VOICE And now Hooters is proud to present Felicity's favorite song, and sung by your very own Maître d', Lonny Jack Hawkins.

They all applaud as the Voice/Maître d' walks into a spotlight upstage and starts to sing in a lush, pleasing voice.

Reverend Mike and Hildegarde, and Luella and Leonard, return to dancing with the music.

VOICE/MAÎTRE D' (*singing*)
Dancing in the dark, 'til the tune ends
We're dancing in the dark, and it soon ends
We're waltzing in the wonder of why we're here
Time hurries by, we're here, and we're gone

During the next section, Voice/Maître d' sings the melody on "la la la" instead of with lyrics, and more softly so we can hear the dialogue.

Lights take us to Felicity and Zamir at the bar.

FELICITY It is my favorite song. Do you remember Fred Astaire and Cyd Charisse dancing to it?

ZAMIR No, I don't.

FELICITY They were a lovely couple. (*hums along a bit*)

VOICE/MAÎTRE D' (*sings*)
We're waltzing in the wonder of why we're here
Time hurries by, we're here and we're gone
(*switches again to singly softly and on "la"*)
La la la la la, la la la la la la la

Back to Zamir and Felicity, who are watching the dancers.

ZAMIR So, we still haven't decided. Should we stay and have a date? Or should we go our separate ways?

FELICITY It's hard to know. It's safer if you just never meet my father. And it's not just him, though. Can you . . . Ummm . . .

ZAMIR Be a different person?

FELICITY I want to believe you can be the same person, but with better aspects.

ZAMIR You're a dreamer.

FELICITY Oddly, I believe people can change. (*sadly*) Just most don't. I don't know if you should go or stay.

ZAMIR Yeah, me neither.

FELICITY What was that thing you said before that I liked?

ZAMIR I don't want to laugh at your dreams?

FELICITY Yes, that was nice . . . you know, the music is pretty. Maybe we should dance and decide afterward. Okay?

ZAMIR I'm not a good dancer.

FELICITY Me neither. But it's just walking slow really.

ZAMIR (*friendly*) Okay.

FELICITY (*smiles*) Okay.

Felicity and Zamir get up and join the other two couples dancing. The mirror ball continues to spin and throw light all around. The Voice/Maître d' returns to singing in a fuller voice. The music sounds sweeping and romantic.

VOICE/MAÎTRE D' (*sings*)
Looking for the light of a new love
To brighten up the night, I have you, love
And we can face the music together
Dancing in the dark, dancing in the dark
Dancing in the dark . . . .

The three couples keep dancing. End of play.

Excerpts from
Sex and Longing

AUTHOR'S NOTE

I wrote a play in 1995 and 1996 called *Sex and Longing*. I envisioned it as an epic play in a nonrealistic style in which the lives of two anarchic sex addicts become entangled with a hypocritical senator, his rigidly religious wife, and a televangelist reverend. There was an early reading of the play's first draft that was way too long, but seemed nonetheless to engage the audience and have an unusual scope to it.

The play was given a strong production by Lincoln Center in 1996, and had four remarkable performances by Sigourney Weaver, Dana Ivey, Guy Boyd, and Peter Michael Goetz. (My colleague John Guare told me he thought Ms. Ivey gave a "classic comic performance" in the role of the senator's wife. She was truly hilarious.)

The play got harsh reviews, but it was part of the Lincoln Center subscription, so the audiences kept coming anyway. I found myself proud of the first two acts, which mostly played well. The third act, though, seemed to lose its way in the writing; I could feel it in the way the audience started to disengage or get restless. So I have never had it published because I think the play goes off in the last third.

However, I find a lot of it funny; and the play is also definitely political in its obsession and frustration with the religious right. Though written in 1996, it seems pretty current to me in its themes. As a lapsed Catholic, I have had to think through and walk away from many of the beliefs I had as a child and young adult. And I find it upsetting over the past several decades how various religious beliefs and opinions keep being entangled with government and laws.

So for the purposes of this book, I am including several scenes from the play. When I skip ahead, I offer brief explanations to take you to the next scene.

Sex and Longing was first produced by Lincoln Center Theater (André Bishop, Bernard Gerstein, directors) at the Cort Theater in New York City on September 12, 1996, and opened on October 10, 1996. It was directed by Garland Wright; sets were designed by John Arnone, costumes by Susan Hilferty, lighting by Brian MacDevitt, sound by John Gromada, company manager was Rheba Flegelman, stage manager was Dianne Trulock. Understudies were Felicity LaFortune, Bill Dawes, Michael Arkin, Cynthia Darlow. The cast was:

Lulu	Sigourney Weaver
Justin	Jay Goede
Senator Harry McCrea	Guy Boyd
Bridget McCrea	Dana Ivey
Reverend Davidson	Peter Michael Goetz
Policeman/Jack/Special Witness	Eric Thal

CHARACTERS

LULU

Attractive woman, age 34 to 42. Sexually driven, confused, vulnerable.

JUSTIN

Her friend and roommate, age 28 to 34. Also sexually driven, but not as much as Lulu. Sense of humor, playful.

SENATOR HARRY McCULLOCH

United States senator, age 35–45. Likeable at core, though unfocused and no real beliefs. Says what he thinks will get him elected. On the side picks up prostitutes a lot.

BRIDGET McCULLOCH

The senator's conservative wife, age 35 to 45. Extremely forceful and critical. Raised as a Catholic, she believes in the Church's dictums so strongly, she cannot even begin to fathom anyone else's beliefs. Definitely believes what she says.

REVEREND DAVIDSON

Nationally known clergyman, age 45 to 60. Impressive, authoritative. He has his own religious TV program.

POLICEMAN

Silent part. Cop who meets Justin.

JACK

A serial killer who meets Lulu.

SURPRISE WITNESS

Brings an otherworldly perspective to a televised congressional hearing.

NOTE: Policeman, Jack, and Surprise Witness are played by the same actor.

ACT I

SCENE I

A loft in Washington, D.C. There is very little furniture. A large unmade bed. A few chairs.

LULU, *an extremely beautiful woman in her late 30s or early 40s, is dressed in a slip and is seated in a wooden chair.* JUSTIN, *a rather cute (but probably not handsome) guy in his 20s or 30s, is seated in a more comfortable chair, doing a crossword puzzle.*

In the scene we learn that Lulu and Justin met at a sexual compulsives meeting. They share this loft, but are constantly dashing out to look for sex. Lulu is more driven and emotionally tortured than Justin is. Neither one of them goes to meetings anymore.

This excerpt begins toward the end of the scene.

LULU (*sad, vulnerable*) I'm filled with sex and longing! Sex and longing! It's been 25 minutes since I've had sex, I really can't wait that long. I feel devastated, I feel unwanted, I feel unloved, I feel undesired. Oh, God. What can I do? Is this normal, to want sex every 15 minutes? Church and society tell me "no," but I feel what I feel, and I feel desperate. Sex and longing! Sex and longing! Oh my God, oh my God!

JUSTIN Now, who's talking in paragraphs?

LULU That wasn't a paragraph, that was a prose poem! If you had any sense, you'd recognize a prose poem when you heard it. Oh, Lord. (*screams*) AAAAAAAAAAGGGGGGGGHHHHH! I am so filled with grief and fatigue, and longing. (*to Justin*) I know you're gay, but are you sure you don't want to have sex with me for just a few minutes?

JUSTIN I'm sorry, no. I'm afraid of women physically, the women I grew up with were terrifying, it's just a big whopping block with me. Sorry. Besides, I have my own needs. (*looking at watch*) Three hours is almost up, it's going to be time for me to go find some sex.

LULU You're so lucky you can wait three hours. How do you do it?

JUSTIN Well, I have other interests. You know, I have my own ego, sort of, it functions for a couple of hours at a time, and then I go get sex. Sometimes it's for fun, but mostly it's just longing.

LULU Oh, sex and longing, sex and longing. But I've said that, haven't I? I really can't wait a moment longer. Excuse me.

Lulu grabs a raincoat, puts it on quickly, puts on shoes, and leaves the apartment.

Scene 2

Stage left lights up: it's a street with a bench and a streetlamp. Lulu hangs on to the lamppost, keeps flashing her raincoat open to supposed passers-by.

LULU Hey there! Want some company? (*calls out again*) Hello, out there! I'm not wearing much, and I'm available. Oooooooo. Hello. Oooooooooo. Yummmy. I'm yummy, and I'm available. Ooooooooo.

A MAN *walks by. He is in a suit, and is late 30s to late 40s. He stands near her.*

Hello.

MAN Hello.

LULU Ooooooooooooooooo.

Note*: sound is the "oo" sound in "who."*

MAN I'm sorry?

LULU I said, Ooooooooooooooo. It's just so warm out tonight, and I'm feeling so, well, what word to use: oooooooooooooo.

MAN Yes. I know what you mean. I feel that way too sometimes.

LULU Yes. We're fellow travelers of longing. Oooooooooo.

MAN Yes. Well. Good night. (*starts to leave*)

LULU Wait! Don't go. I'm . . . uh. Got a light?

MAN For what?

LULU Oh, that's right, I don't have a cigarette. If I did, would you have a light?

MAN I might.

LULU Oh, baby, light my fire.

MAN Yeah. That's a good song.

LULU It's a good feeling. Goodness, this is moving sort of slowly. Um. . . . hi, honey. Don't be frightened of me. I'm just out for a bit of a loiter. I'm loitering with intent. I suppose it's not normal, but what's normal? Salmon swim upstream to be eaten by bears, is that normal? And yet they do it. You wanna swim upstream with me? Ooooooooooooooooo.

MAN I wouldn't mind a . . .

LULU . . . fuck?

MAN I was going to say "swim."

LULU I'm sorry, I shouldn't use bad language. I think bad things, but I shouldn't say them. But I think them. (*opens up her raincoat, flaps it around*) I need air. I'm just so warm and . . . liquid . . . and I just feel like some . . . (*Southern accent*) . . . "companionship." I like to say that word with a Southern accent because it makes it more genteel, and you can just feel the soft air coming in off the sea breezes. Soft air caressing my bare skin, I have bare skin underneath this slip. Do you want to swim upstream and be eaten by my bare skin?

MAN Yes, I would. How much?

LULU Oh, honey, I don't charge money, I give it away. It's a gift to give. You have a gift to give me. I'm tremendously . . . well, horny is really the wrong word. I'm desperate. I feel tremendously empty, I have a chasm of longing screeching inside me. I hope that doesn't frighten you off. It actually just makes me very passionate in lovemaking. You don't really sense any neurosis in me unless you go out for coffee afterward or something, and I recommend that you don't. I want to give myself to you. Am I coming on too strong? You look sort of alarmed.

MAN No, I guess I'd just feel better if I could pay you.

LULU You could make a donation to one of my favorite charities.

MAN I'm married, you know. This is a picture of my wife. (*shows it*)

LULU Oh, she's hideous, I don't like her at all. Unless you were suggesting a threesome, but I don't think you were.

MAN Are you bisexual?

LULU If it would please you.

MAN I don't like bisexuality. I think it's abnormal.

LULU Abnormal. Uh, these concepts just elude me. Gosh, we're talking so long, and we're not making love. Oooooooooo. Ahhhhhhhhhh. Eeeeeeeeee.

MAN What?

LULU Come on, baby, come on-a my house.

MAN You're so sexy.

Lulu drags him back to her apartment.

In the apartment scene that follows, the Man becomes uncomfortable. He's bothered Justin is there, though Justin is willing to leave. But Lulu's needy enthusiasm scares the Man off and he leaves. Lulu is devastated. Her emotions go up and down all the time.

Later on we see the Man who picked up Lulu as he returns to his house the same night.

SCENE 5

The bedroom of the Man who had previously been with Lulu. Twin beds.

In bed is his wife, BRIDGET, *late 30s to late 40s. She wears a very old-fashioned, buttoned-up, unappealing nightgown. It has a K-mart femininity, but she is strong and no-nonsense and relentless.*

The man's name is HARRY McCREA *He is still in his suit, but he looks a little disheveled. He is tiptoeing in, hoping not to wake Bridget, but no such luck.*

BRIDGET Harry, where have you been?

HARRY I had to work late. We're working on an appropriations bill.

BRIDGET It's 4 in the morning.

HARRY I'm a senator. I take my responsibilities seriously.

BRIDGET I called your office. There was no one there.

HARRY I was there till late, then I took a walk, thinking about our country and what's the matter with it.

BRIDGET People like you are what's the matter with it.

HARRY Yes, thank you. Hello to you too.

BRIDGET What time did you leave the Senate?

HARRY What time did you call?

BRIDGET What time did you leave, Harry?

HARRY I didn't look at my watch. What time did you call?

BRIDGET I called at 12:30, after midnight.

HARRY Ah, well, I left just before midnight, and I've just been walking. I've been having Senate thoughts.

BRIDGET And you were there before 12:30?

HARRY Yes, I was.

BRIDGET I called at 11, and you weren't there.

HARRY Oh, this is pointless, just go to sleep.

BRIDGET Is that lipstick I see on your collar?

HARRY No, it isn't. On my zipper perhaps, but not my collar.

BRIDGET What did you say?

HARRY I said absolutely nothing. Now why don't you please go to sleep.

BRIDGET This is nothing like my parents' marriage. My father worshipped my mother.

HARRY How nice for her. Did he actually kneel and light candles, or do you mean something else?

BRIDGET He respected her as the mother of his children, and as his helpmate through all his life.

HARRY Did your mother hate sex like you do?

BRIDGET Don't try to blame me for your perversions. My parents were above earthly pleasures.

HARRY Well, they had 11 children, they must have done it sometimes.

BRIDGET Don't you defame the memory of my parents.

HARRY How is it defaming them to say they had sex?

BRIDGET And they both had a strong faith. They believed in Jesus Christ and the pope, and they went to Mass every Sunday and every holy day. And every other day as well.

HARRY Well, I'm sorry your life doesn't seem to you like your parents'. Maybe you should have been born in 1910.

BRIDGET People had values then.

HARRY Uh-huh.

BRIDGET You weren't this way when I married you. You came from a fine Catholic family.

HARRY Yeah, yeah, yeah.

BRIDGET I should have married your brother Terrence.

HARRY Priests can't marry.

BRIDGET I mean, if he hadn't become a priest. He's obviously the good one in your family.

HARRY He likes little boys.

BRIDGET Oh, you're disgusting. I'm sure it's not true.

HARRY Don't you read the paper? He was arrested and sent to prison.

BRIDGET Of course, I don't read the paper. I read the *Catholic Digest,* and I subscribe to Reverend Davidson's newsletter, the In Deep Sorrow at the State of Human Morality Society Monthly Bulletin. I bought you a subscription for the office. Do you ever read it?

HARRY I don't know. Maybe when I'm on the toilet.

BRIDGET Don't be disgusting.

HARRY Everything about the body disgusts you.

BRIDGET It's meant to disgust you. The body is the temptation of the devil. God wants you to use your body for the holy sacrament of marriage, and for the creation of children, and then that's *it* for the body.

HARRY I would like to go unconscious now please.

BRIDGET I don't know what happened. You were a good man when I met you. You seemed so happy when we had our first child. Then you changed. The devil got into you, or some secret drive that you won't extinguish. I pray every night that God will make you different.

HARRY Thank you. I'm going to sleep on the couch.

BRIDGET No. Don't sleep on the couch. We're married for life, Harry. Even if we hate one another, we're bound together. Get into bed, Harry. I'll just pretend you're not here. But we must do what's proper.

HARRY Mmmmmmmm. All right. I'll pretend you're not here too.

Lights fade on them.

Later in the play we learn that Lulu and Justin have written and published a pornographic coffee table book called *Explicit Photographs of the Last 300 People We Slept With,* and this has given them a small income.

The book has come to the horrified attention of Bridget, who reaches out to a famous conservative televangelist named Reverend Davidson. The following is a section of their scene together.

SCENE 8

The sitting room of the REVEREND DAVIDSON.

Nice furnishings, though a bit grandiose. A large, life-size crucifix with the suffering body of Christ on it dominates the room. It is enormous.

The Reverend is on his knees praying. He is distinguished-looking.

REVEREND DAVIDSON

And lead us not into temptation,
But deliver us from evil,
For thine is the kingdom and the power and the glory,
For ever and ever . . .

Enter Bridget.

BRIDGET Reverend Davidson, your housekeeper said you were ready to see me.

REVEREND DAVIDSON Oh yes. (*gets up from his knees*) Mrs. McCrea. How nice to meet you. And thank you for your kind letter.

BRIDGET Thank you. As I said, I've admired your work. And I love your newsletter. It expresses exactly how I feel. (*a bit overwhelmed by the large crucifix*) Goodness, that's such a large crucifix.

REVEREND DAVIDSON Does it disturb you?

BRIDGET No. Of course not. It's quite beautiful. It just overwhelms me rather. It reminds me of our Savior's suffering, and how responsible we are for his pain.

REVEREND DAVIDSON Yes. We are.

BRIDGET And how even more responsible for his pain are the other people in the world who commit sin after sin after sin.

REVEREND DAVIDSON Yes, indeed. Now, I was interested when you wrote me that your husband was Senator Harold McCrea and that you thought he might be able to help me in my ministry.

BRIDGET Yes, I do. Harold was elected on a very conservative ticket, and he's a good man, he . . . has his flaws, he's not as morally good as he should be, we're sad about our children, we have 5 children, 2 of them have turned out beautifully, they're our pride and joy, and two of them are so-so, I don't know how moral they are, and the youngest one is well, he's in trouble a lot, you know, the school calls up and says they want to expel him, we don't know what to do with Kenny. And then there's Patrick. He's dead. He was the oldest. It's very sad. He was drinking, I think there may have been marijuana, and he took pills. It's a sadness.

REVEREND DAVIDSON So you've suffered in your life, Mrs. McCrea.

BRIDGET Yes, I have. Patrick was a lovely child, but it turns out he grew up to be one of those . . . you know.

REVEREND DAVIDSON I'm sorry. He grew up to be . . .

BRIDGET Well, he had a problem with sexuality. They used to say if the mother was too strong and the father was too weak that then the child could grow up to be . . . you know, to like people like himself. And, of course, that's a very sad thing. And the Bible speaks against it many times.

REVEREND DAVIDSON He was homosexual.

BRIDGET Please, that word hurts my ears. I feel momentarily nauseous. Let me put my head between my knees for a moment. (*She does this.*)

REVEREND DAVIDSON Can I offer you refreshment?

BRIDGET No, it'll pass. (*brings her head up again*)

You know, we made it clear to Patrick that it wasn't him we hated, it was his sin that we hated. We urged him to move back home. To join us for holy holidays. Christmas, Thanksgiving. We wore rubber gloves around him, and masks on our faces, because we didn't know if he had that disease or not. I mean, not all of them do, I know that, but we had to protect ourselves.

REVEREND DAVIDSON Yes, of course, a great sadness.

BRIDGET He left a note. It didn't blame us. It just said, "I hate life." But we had taught him to love life. And love God.

REVEREND DAVIDSON You say you wore masks. But he was not, to your knowledge, HIV-positive?

BRIDGET Who can say? He didn't look ill, although he had a little earring in his ear. It's a great sorrow. I barely know how to get over it. And now my youngest one, Kenny. He's a mess.

REVEREND DAVIDSON Does your husband help with the children?

BRIDGET Oh, my husband. Well, he used to be very moral, his brother is a priest. He's in prison now, I guess, but . . . never mind that. But my husband—I don't know *what* he believes in anymore.

REVEREND DAVIDSON He's fallen away from the faith of his fathers?

BRIDGET Yes he has. But you see, he can be manipulated, he can be made to vote on things you and I believe in because he wants to be reelected, and the voters want a stronger sense of morality in our country.

REVEREND DAVIDSON Yes, they do.

BRIDGET As I do. I *long* for morality. My parents had a beautiful marriage, my father worshipped my mother. Everything made sense in the past. In the country, we acted as one. We fought in World War II as one; we stood up against the communists as one. We moved to the suburbs as one. We knew what was right and wrong, and we taught it to our children. I mean, on the penny it says, "In God We Trust," right?

REVEREND DAVIDSON Right, indeed.

BRIDGET So God should be in our thoughts. He's on our pennies. But now! I say we should get busy! And use my husband to pass laws that reinforce and monitor morality. I mean, there are naked bodies on the television. When I was little, Lucille Ball was on the television. I want to return to those days.

REVEREND DAVIDSON Lucille Ball is dead.

BRIDGET Yes, but luckily, her reruns are available. And I want them to rerun Bishop Sheen. Do you remember him? He was this wonderful Catholic bishop who gave sermons on television every Sunday night right after Ed Sullivan. I want him on television again.

REVEREND DAVIDSON Bishop Sheen and Ed Sullivan are also dead.

BRIDGET My point exactly! The good people are dead.

Bridget and the Reverend look sad at this truth.

As the scene continues, Bridget shows the Reverend the explicit coffee table book Justin and Lulu have written. They decide they will encourage Bridget's senator husband to conduct a congressional investigation of this book.

SCENE 9

The hearings. A room in the Senate.

Senator Harry McCrea is at a table with a microphone in front of him.

Next to him is a large blow-up doll with an open mouth, the kind bought at porno stores. The doll is seated upright in a chair.

Sitting across from Harry, also behind a small table with a microphone, is Justin.

The microphone in front of Senator Harry is enormous. The microphone in front of Justin is very small.

Harry bangs a gavel.

HARRY (*speaks into microphone*) Testing, testing. Is this thing on?
At the request of my wife, my wonderful, extremely moral wife, I am now calling to order the Senate subcommittee on Obscenity in the Literary Arts. (*referring to the blow-up doll*) My distinguished colleague, the attractive Senator Barbara Fellatio, from the randy state of Wyoming, is my co-chair. We welcome the first witness, Justin Fellatio. Strange, you both have the same last name.

JUSTIN Senator, my last name is not Fellatio. It is Stewart. Justin Stewart.

HARRY Uh-huh. I see. Let me write that down. (*writes*) Last name is not Fellatio. (*back to Justin*) And with a Miss Lulu DuBois, you are the author of this book *Explicit Photographs of the Last 300 People We Slept With*?

JUSTIN Yes, I am.

HARRY (*hearing something from the doll*) What? (*puts his ear near the doll's face, listens*) I see. I'm sorry. (*back to Justin*) My distinguished colleague, Senator Barbara Fellatio from the randy state of Wyoming, has just informed me that her last name is not Fellatio either. What is your last name, Senator? (*listens*) Cunnilingus, but spelled with a "K." Most unusual name. Is it Irish? But that would be O'Cunnilingus. Maybe she's Polish.

JUSTIN Senator, may I request a reality check? Is the senator from Wyoming on your right actually a senator, or is she indeed a blow-up doll such as one might buy in a porno store?

HARRY Exactly! So you've been to a porno store! Tell me about it.

JUSTIN Well, you go in, and there are large dildos on the wall.

HARRY Yes, yes, that's been my experience too.

JUSTIN Then on all the walls there are these rows and rows of magazines, all with men and women, and women and women, and men and men, all doing things with their genitals and so on and so forth.

HARRY Uh huh. I think the senator has a question. (*listens to the doll; then speaks to Justin*) Have you ever seen a blow-up doll in one of these establishments that was a male doll?

JUSTIN Yes, I have.

HARRY And do you think that this male doll would be interested in meeting the distinguished senator from Wyoming?

JUSTIN (*knows it's crazy but feels he should answer something*) Yes, possibly. Senator, I'm confused why your committee has subpoenaed me here today.

HARRY Your name was given to me by my wife. She and the Reverend Davidson have brought to this committee's attention your rather startling and entertaining coffee table book, *Explicit Photographs of the Last 300 People We Slept With.*

JUSTIN Oh, you found it entertaining?

HARRY I'm sorry, I didn't mean entertaining, I meant disgusting. Please let the record show that I said the word "disgusting," not "entertaining."

JUSTIN Perhaps "entertaining" was a Freudian slip.

HARRY No, it wasn't. Freud himself said that sometimes a cigar was just a cigar and not a penis. Strike that last mention of the word "penis." Let the record show I said nothing after the word "cigar." Mr. Fellatio, do you ever smoke a cigar?

JUSTIN I'm sorry, my name is not Fellatio.

HARRY That's right, it's Cunnilingus with a "K." No, that's the senator.

JUSTIN Is the doll on your right indeed a senator?

HARRY Yes, she is. Her triumphant election was the result of the anti-incumbency mood throughout the country. In Wyoming the incumbent was a senator of 35 years' distinguished service, but the voters got irritated and they voted for this life-size plastic doll instead. And we in the Senate are doing our best to honor the choice of the state of Wyoming. And to honor ourselves. And our constitution. Speaking of which, I suppose you're going to bore us all by saying that this filthy book you've written is protected by your First Amendment right to free speech.

JUSTIN Yes, I would like to bore you with that sentiment. Besides, it isn't pornography if there is redeeming social value of any sort.

HARRY You know, as one of the Supreme Court justices said, I can't define pornography, but I know it when I see it. And if it gives me an erection, I consider it pornography. I'm sorry, please strike that last remark from the record.

JUSTIN No one is forced to buy or look at my book, Senator.

HARRY Uh-huh. (*listens to doll*) What? (*to Justin*) She's telling me a dirty joke. (*listens*) Uh-huh. Uh-huh. Something about a proctologist and lost car keys. Very funny. I love proctologist jokes. And I love social security. I'll never cut it.

JUSTIN Senator, I don't understand what the committee wants of me.

HARRY I don't either. My wife is really behind this. Dear, why don't you come out here and help a moment, would you?

Enter Bridget and the Reverend Davidson. They sit at the table but are a little hesitant about joining the committee.

BRIDGET I haven't really been elected.

HARRY Yes, but the people love you. Come sit down. Reverend Davidson, you too.

REVEREND DAVIDSON I hope if I sit on the committee, there's no problem with the separation of church and state.

HARRY Not with me, there isn't.

BRIDGET I mean, religious people have rights too.

HARRY Exactly. I turn the questions over to my wife. I will work out figures to balance the national budget, while she focuses on your disgusting book.

BRIDGET Mr. Stewart . . .

HARRY His name is Fellatio, dear.

BRIDGET What?

JUSTIN No, no, your wife is right. Stewart.

HARRY Sorry, I'll stay out of it. Call him what you want. I'll do my calculations. (*takes out small book and calculator; makes notations*)

BRIDGET Mr. Stewart, do you pretend that your revolting book has any redeeming social value?

JUSTIN Well, the quality of the images is artistic. The posing of the various genitals is thoughtfully done. The introduction by Camille Paglia uses words and concepts and thoughts, and thus is considered to be of social value.

BRIDGET Well, I am deeply offended. I do not wish to look at pictures of genitals.

JUSTIN Then don't look at them.

BRIDGET And I don't want anyone else to look at them.

JUSTIN Well, why is that your business?

BRIDGET Christ said, "Am I not my brother's keeper?" I must follow Christ.

JUSTIN I see.

BRIDGET Let me ask this: have you ever used any taxpayer funds to support this revolting assault on society's morals?

JUSTIN No, I haven't.

The Reverend Davidson whispers to Bridget.

BRIDGET Mr. Stewart, have you ever received a tax rebate of any kind?

JUSTIN Yes. Once I worked as a bookkeeper for a ballet company, and for that tax year I received a refund of $76.

BRIDGET How do we know that you have not saved that $76 of our tax monies . . .

JUSTIN Well, my tax money . . .

BRIDGET No, it came from the government . . . and that you've used that $76 to pay for some or all of this obscene document?

JUSTIN Well, it's not "tax money," it's a rebate, it's my money being given back to me.

BRIDGET I don't think that's correct. Harry, you're the expert in finances. Could you respond to this?

HARRY (*looking up from his notebook*) If we execute all people over age 70, we can balance the budget without having to cut any of social security.

BRIDGET Dear, this isn't the time to balance the budget. We're talking about morality here. This man may have used a tax rebate to support his writing this offensive book.

HARRY Oh, he did? Well fie on you, Mr. Fellatio Head. You make me sick.

JUSTIN A tax rebate is my own money.

HARRY That's not my understanding of tax rebate. A tax rebate, in some circumstances, can be a euphemism for a grant from liberals at the National Endowment for the Arts for the purpose of creating and fostering obscenity in American society.

BRIDGET Exactly.

JUSTIN Well, I don't mean that kind of a tax rebate.

HARRY Well, that's what you say, but you could be lying. How often do you have sex?

JUSTIN Every 3 hours.

HARRY That's amazing. Every 3 hours. I envy you. I only get it about every 15 days, usually with a prostitute.

BRIDGET Harry.

HARRY Uh-oh. Another Freudian slip. I didn't say anything about a prostitute. You know what? I think I'd like to get a breath of fresh air. And maybe have some phone sex.

BRIDGET Harry!

HARRY I'm sorry, I mean balance the budget. You finish this thing on obscenity, all right? (*exits hurriedly*)

BRIDGET Mr. Stewart, tell me, whose idea was it to write your obscene book, you or your coauthor, Miss DuBois?

JUSTIN I don't remember. We were just taking pictures of people and Lulu said, wouldn't this make a nice coffee table book?

REVEREND DAVIDSON If I may, I think we should call in Miss DuBois and interrogate her ourselves.

BRIDGET I agree. Mr. Stewart, you are released for the present.

REVEREND DAVIDSON Please send the next witness in: Miss DuBois.

Before Justin can leave, Lulu comes in.

LULU Fuck me! Fuck me!

REVEREND DAVIDSON Please, do not speak in obscenities!

LULU Oh, Reverend Davidson, hello. Are you ready to sleep with me yet?

REVEREND DAVIDSON Don't be disgusting.

LULU I've only had it five times today. I feel positively desperate.

REVEREND DAVIDSON Mr. Stewart, you are excused. Miss DuBois, pull yourself together.

JUSTIN I'll be outside, Lulu. (*exits*)

LULU It's been two whole hours. I tried to masturbate, but I couldn't get interested in myself at all. I need another person to react to me.

REVEREND DAVIDSON Will you stop speaking in obscenities please!

LULU I'm sorry, did I speak in an obscenity? You'll have to excuse me. I have no idea how to behave. I am unmoored.

REVEREND DAVIDSON What?

LULU I am unmoored. I have lost my mooring . . . you know, a boat is moored to the dock, but if the rope breaks it drifts and drifts . . . I have no idea how to live or how to behave. Anyone want to sleep with me? I'm available! I'll do it for a smile, or a frown, makes no difference to me!

REVEREND DAVIDSON Please, we're on C-SPAN. Now state your name for the record please.

LULU Lulu. Lulu DuBois. It means white woods in French. French is the language of love. And the language of tongue. French kissing is tongue kissing. It's very intimate to put your tongue in someone's mouth.

REVEREND DAVIDSON Name, name, just say your name.

LULU Lulu DuBois.

REVEREND DAVIDSON I thought your name was Sadie Thompson.

LULU I changed it.

REVEREND DAVIDSON Miss Thompson—are you aware that you have an eternal soul?

LULU I have heard of my eternal soul, and sometimes I have a feeling that it is there. But I am not certain. I'm very busy much of the time. Every fifteen minutes, you know. (*looks at her watch*) You seem to be the only man in the room. Although if we're on C-SPAN, there's probably a cameraman somewhere. (*calls out*) Oh, cameraman, I can't see you, but I bet you're very attractive. Fuck me!

REVEREND DAVIDSON Miss Thompson! You are a disgrace.

Senator Harry enters.

HARRY Where is this Miss DuBois person?

LULU Oh, a man. You look familiar.

HARRY You do too. I think I went to your apartment.

LULU You did?

HARRY No, I don't know what I'm saying. I've never seen you, I'll swear on a stack on Bibles. I think I'll go again. (*exits*)

LULU He's gone. Oh, dear. Come back, I'm available. Yoo-hoo!

REVEREND DAVIDSON There seem to be no limits to your debauchery, Miss Thompson.

LULU There are limits.

REVEREND DAVIDSON What are they?

LULU Time. Geography. When I pass out from exhaustion.

REVEREND DAVIDSON There should be more limits than that.

LULU Reverend Davidson, I'm not wearing anything under this sheet.

REVEREND DAVIDSON I am happy to tell you that under my clothes I am wearing a suit of armor. And under that I am wearing fire-engine red long underwear. And under that, pasted to my skin, are pages from the Bible. I come well prepared to face you, Whore of Babylon.

LULU Where is Babylon? Isn't that in Long Island?

REVEREND DAVIDSON Sadie Thompson, the Feminists Against Pornography say that your book degrades women. Although in most cases I find the feminist movement irritating, when they don't like pornographic pictures I very much agree with them.

LULU Will there be any other men coming to this meeting?

REVEREND DAVIDSON Sadie Thompson—do you know the purpose of womanhood?

LULU Ummmm . . . well, I don't know. Is there an answer to that question?

REVEREND DAVIDSON Yes, there is. God created Eve from Adam's rib, because Adam was lonely and needed a helpmate.

LULU Uh huh. Isn't that a metaphor . . . being created from a rib? (*looks out, flirting with imagined cameraman*) Oh, cameraman!

REVEREND DAVIDSON The Bible is God's word. If he wanted to speak to us in metaphors, I'm sure He would have. But no, He spoke in clear, unambiguous sentences. Will you stop winking at the cameraman, please? We must follow the Bible, or face eternal damnation.

LULU Uh-huh. I see. Excuse me—are you working for the government, or is this some religious conference?

BRIDGET My husband is a senator. I don't know why he left before, but the distinguished Reverend Davidson is asking questions in his stead. So there is no church-state separation issue here.

REVEREND DAVIDSON Exactly. Thank you, Mrs. McCrea.

LULU Sometimes I sleep with some poor celibate priest, and he's so pent up from years of abstinence that we have a really great time! You might consider it, Reverend.

BRIDGET She's so disgusting!

REVEREND DAVIDSON Miss DuBois, we are here to investigate you as the author of this pornographic, antifamily document.

LULU Where's the senator fellow? Oh, Senator! Senator!

REVEREND DAVIDSON Stop that. Miss DuBois, in this hand I hold your book. And in this hand I hold the Good Book.

LULU My book has pictures.

REVEREND DAVIDSON Indeed it does. In the Good Book we learn that Adam and Eve sinned, and then they were thrown out of the Garden of Paradise.

LULU I miss the Garden of Paradise. I think that's what I'm seeking when I have sex all the time . . . I want to return there.

REVEREND DAVIDSON Sex will not return you to the Garden of Paradise, Sadie Thompson. The Garden of Paradise is no more. Adam and Eve destroyed it by their willfulness.

LULU I hate them for that. I would have liked to have lived there, and to have named the animals with them. Oh, look, let's call that a Doberman pinscher. Oh, look, there's a schnauzer. (*suddenly anxious*) Oh my God, is this interrogation over? I needed to find sex two hours ago!!!!!

BRIDGET Reverend, it's hard for me to remain silent. May I speak to Miss DuBois?

REVEREND DAVIDSON Yes, go ahead, Mrs. McCrea.

BRIDGET Miss DuBois, you've written a disgusting book, and you live a disgusting life, fornicating every fifteen minutes apparently, and children around America will look at you and copy you, and I am appalled by this. I am concerned about America. The people don't have morals or values. So I speak up about it, and I tell what the truth is. The Bible speaks the truth; it is the objective word of God. Why don't you follow it?

LULU Okay, I'll follow it from now on. Can I go now?

BRIDGET Wait, I'm not finished. He who doesn't know history is doomed to repeat it. Immorality is what brought the Roman Empire down, and I plan to see that it doesn't happen here.

LULU Can I go now?

BRIDGET Nero, Caligula, brothers and sisters sleeping together. I saw *I, Claudius* on public television, and I wish I hadn't. And public television! They use my tax money, and they put things on it that I don't agree with!

LULU How much tax do you pay exactly?

BRIDGET Well, enough to know I don't want it misused by public television. And have you noticed how many programs they put on about these homo/"you know" people, I don't like to say the word. And I had a son who was homo-you-know, and he killed himself because people like you and the executives at PBS don't follow the teachings of Saint Paul, and so children get confused and they sin and they kill themselves.

I think we would all benefit from firing all the PBS executives and replacing them with men who have children, so we know for sure they're normal. Then no more dramatic programs, but just lots of good healthy symphonies playing concerts. I don't like classical music, it stirs you up if you listen to it, but I like to watch the musicians play, I just turn off the sound. I like anything with music, as long as the sound is off. And I want there to be a law against rap music. They tried it in Florida, but some stupid jury said the rap music wasn't obscene. I'd like to be on one of these juries, and I'd tell people what was obscene.

LULU Please, I have to go look for sex. I'M IN PAIN!

BRIDGET I'm in pain too, Miss DuBois.

LULU In what way are you in pain?

BRIDGET I'm in pain the way Jesus Christ is in pain. That the world has fallen so far off the track.

LULU Jesus Christ had compassion for people in pain. Maybe he'll come back and heal me.

BRIDGET I'd like you to be healed. Why don't you let the Reverend Davidson help bring you to Jesus?

LULU And will I be happy if I'm brought to Jesus?

BRIDGET Very happy. You'll be just like me. You'll be righteous, you'll be prepared for heaven, you'll eat three square meals a day.

LULU I need to be held.

BRIDGET Babies need to be held. Grown-ups don't need it anymore.

LULU I need to be held. And then I need to be fucked.

LULU storms out.

REVEREND DAVIDSON Miss Thompson, you are not excused from this committee. You are not excused!!!

BRIDGET After the Fall. She is so after the Fall.

REVEREND DAVIDSON What do you mean?

BRIDGET Eating the apple. Talking to the serpent. She is in communication with the devil. I am shaken.

REVEREND DAVIDSON (*looking at the blow-up doll, frowning*) What is this doll here, do you know?

BRIDGET I don't. Could it be a swimming pool float? Or something to hold on to if your plane crashes into the ocean?

REVEREND DAVIDSON I don't know. I find it disturbing.

BRIDGET Everything is disturbing.

Later in the play, Lulu goes off at 3 A.M. to try to find someone to have sex with, and she meets a man who initially seems fine, but turns out to be Jack the Ripper.

He harms her, but she is saved by the Reverend Davidson, who often wanders about in the middle of the night, trying to save the souls of prostitutes. Whether he has other reasons for wandering the streets, we think about later.

In any case, the Reverend brings Lulu to his home to convalesce. Her arms have been harmed and she can't presently move them. She is so grateful for the Reverend's saving her that she has become religious.

The following is from the first scene of act 2. Justin has not known where Lulu is and has now found her at the Reverend's house. The Reverend has been somewhat hostile to Justin, and Lulu has been trying to explain her newfound faith.

The excerpt begins toward the end of Lulu's conversation with Justin. The Reverend Davidson is also there.

ACT II

Excerpt from Scene 1

This excerpt starts late in the scene, after Justin and Lulu have been talking awhile.

The sitting room of the Reverend Davidson. Lulu is in a wheelchair. She can walk, but it's hard for her to balance while she can't move her arms. Justin and Lulu are in conversation. The Reverend Davidson is standing a bit apart but is paying close attention.

LULU I am resplendent with faith now. I have an inner glow. Can you see it?

JUSTIN Yeah, sort of. Well, gosh. Um . . . I don't know how to talk to you anymore.

LULU Use words. Put them in an order that communicates how you feel.

JUSTIN I feel . . . you've become a fanatic.

LULU That's your fear talking.

JUSTIN Well, but before you had to have sex every 15 minutes. And now you can't remember anything, and you have to have religion every 15 minutes.

LULU Not every 15 minutes. Every minute. Every second. God lets me breathe. Watch. (*takes a breath; exhales*) See. I was breathing, but it was God who gave me the power.

JUSTIN Uh-huh. Well, fine.

LULU And you're breathing. And God is giving you your breath.

JUSTIN Yes, well. You know, I still the need to . . . "you know what" every 3 hours, so I really better start to get going . . .

LULU The reverend feels you should be quarantined.

JUSTIN Pardon?

LULU He feels you're a danger to yourself and others. You're bound to spread AIDS . . . not to mention sin.

JUSTIN I don't have AIDS. I practice safe sex . . . mostly.

LULU Perhaps you don't have AIDS today, but . . .

REVEREND DAVIDSON Sin, sin. The body is a gift from God, and we defile it.

LULU Yes, we do. Or did. Justin, the reverend can help you.

REVEREND DAVIDSON Yes, I can. I have had a lot of success with homosexuals who now are either celibate, or who are in stable heterosexual marriages, or who are in mental hospitals, but for whom we have high hope of happiness in heaven.

JUSTIN Look, I have different beliefs than you.

REVEREND DAVIDSON God created Adam and Eve, not Adam and Steve.

JUSTIN What an extremely brilliant remark. You should get it copyrighted.

REVEREND DAVISON Not Adam and Steve. Not Adam and Bruce. Not Adam and Fifi, where Fifi is a drag queen performer.

JUSTIN Lulu . . . I've got to go. I hope the muscles in your arms heal. I'm glad you weren't killed.

LULU Good-bye, Justin. The reverend and I will pray for you.

JUSTIN I don't mind if you pray. I can do without the reverend's prayers.

REVEREND DAVIDSON Nonetheless, I shall pray for you, young man.

Bridget enters, slightly dressed up.

BRIDGET Your housekeeper said I could just come in. (*sees Justin*) Oh, my.

REVEREND DAVIDSON Mrs. McCrea, this is Justin Stuart, the Sodomite. We interrogated him on his filthy book.

BRIDGET Oh, yes. Today he looks like my son. The dead one. May I sit down? I feel dizzy.

REVEREND DAVIDSON (*to Justin*) I'm afraid you'll have to leave now. We're about to teach Sadie Thompson the art of having a normal conversation, and I do not feel you can participate in this.

JUSTIN Fine. Good-bye.

LULU Good-bye, Justin. Be happy for me.

JUSTIN Yes, good-bye. (*half to himself*) I'm going to do my best to forget this meeting. I think I may need to go have sex with about 20 people right away. Yuck. (*exits*)

BRIDGET He has the same expression in his eyes that my son had. It was upsetting.

LULU Justin is very sweet.

REVEREND DAVIDSON I didn't see the sweetness. I only saw the immortality. Well, in time he may come to his senses. But if he doesn't . . . we are working on the quarantine laws. Perhaps we can save him from himself.

LULU Yes. The way you saved me.

REVEREND DAVIDSON Are you grateful, Sadie Thompson?

LULU Yes, I am.

REVEREND DAVIDSON Good. Gratefulness bespeaks humility. And humility is when we know we are worthless, and powerless, in the face of God.

LULU Oh, I'm worthless?

REVEREND DAVIDSON Compared to God, you are.

LULU Oh, yes, right. I'm worthless compared to God.

REVEREND DAVIDSON Mrs. McCrea, I'm so pleased you're here today. Are you here?

BRIDGET (*having been lost in thought*) Yes. Sorry. That young man . . . upset me.

REVEREND DAVIDSON He's an upsetting young man. Mrs. McCrea, I don't believe you're seen Miss Thompson, my spiritual daughter, since she found God.

BRIDGET No, I haven't. She certainly looks better. Well, not the wheelchair, of course, but before she was in a sheet or something, wasn't she?

LULU I am so grateful to be alive. God gives me every breath I breathe.

BRIDGET Me too. (*laughs*)

REVEREND DAVIDSON Did the housekeeper give you the tea tray to bring in?

BRIDGET No. She seemed drunk, actually.

REVEREND DAVIDSON Yes. She has that problem. I should fire her, but I'm tenderhearted.

BRIDGET Well, it's a good man's failing.

REVEREND DAVIDSON Thank you. Did you hear that exchange, Sadie Thompson? We spoke of a situation, and we exchanged generalized feelings of sadness about it, and then Mrs. McCrea offered me a generalized compliment about my goodness. This is a good example of social conversation. Can you learn from it?

LULU I can try.

REVEREND DAVIDSON Mrs. McCrea, would you do me the great favor of going to see the housekeeper and bringing in the tea tray?

BRIDGET Oh. Yes, certainly. I hope it isn't too heavy.

REVEREND DAVIDSON God will help you.

Bridget exits.

LULU I feel nervous. I don't think she likes me. Women usually don't like me.

REVEREND DAVIDSON It's because you're so beautiful. Women are jealous. You must be kind to them because they feel jealous in your presence.

LULU Oh. All right. I'll try.

Bridget comes back with the tea tray.

BRIDGET I found it. It was just sitting out there. I wonder if the tea has gotten cold.

LULU Hello, Mrs. McCrea. Isn't your dress attractive? Not attractive, I don't mean that you're trying to be alluring. Just that you look appropriate. And the dress looks clean. I'm sorry, I don't think I did that well.

REVEREND DAVIDSON It was too complicated. And you'd already said hello. You could have said: Mrs. McCrea, how kind of you to have carried the tea. The muscles in my arm have been severed, so I surely would have dropped it.

LULU Yes, that's a good suggestion. How kind you got the tea. I would have dropped it. My arms don't work.

BRIDGET Yes, I heard what happened to you. Very upsetting.

LULU Very upsetting.

REVEREND DAVIDSON Now let us begin officially. We are now having a social conversation. Let us begin. (*to Bridget*) I'm so glad you could come to formal tea today, Mrs. McCrea.

BRIDGET I'm so happy to be here, Reverend Davidson.

REVEREND DAVIDSON Miss Thompson has been with me a week now. And as part of Miss Thompson's getting well, I wanted to introduce her to the art of social intercourse.

BRIDGET (*a bit alarmed*) What?

REVEREND DAVIDSON Social intercourse. Small talk. Making pleasantries. It's one of the things that makes life bearable. Miss Thompson has lost the knack. She's been no better than a prostitute for years and years.

LULU I never charged my money, I . . .

REVEREND DAVIDSON (*screams*) YOU DID FILTHY, DISGUSTING THINGS, YOU WERE LOWER THAN AN ANIMAL, YOU HAVE TO BE TAUGHT HOW TO REENTER SOCIETY. YOU HAVE BEEN BENEATH CONTEMPT!

LULU Yes, I have. I'm sorry. You're right.

REVEREND DAVIDSON Yes, I am. I'm right. You have known about sexual intercourse, but not social intercourse. Now we will rebegin the social intercourse. Mrs. McCrea, will you restart please?

Pause. Bridget is a bit uncomfortable, thinks a bit, then starts to converse.

BRIDGET Yes. Certainly. The weather is so lovely today

REVEREND DAVIDSON Yes. Very lovely weather.

BRIDGET I so like a day where the sun is shining and the sky is bright.

REVEREND DAVIDSON Yes. It reminds me of the goodness of God.

BRIDGET Yes. (*looks at Lulu*) Should she be made to say something?

REVEREND DAVIDSON Miss Thompson.

LULU I'm sorry. Something about the weather.

BRIDGET Well, I was only saying it was nice out.

LULU Uh-huh. Oh. I was remembering something. Let me not remember. Stop, stop. (*stops the memory*) Uh. I stopped it. Thank goodness.

REVEREND DAVIDSON Goodness is the force of God in our present lives.

LULU Yes. I agree. I'm sorry. Could you scratch my nose for me?

Reverend Davidson gets up, crosses to Lulu, and very methodically scratches her nose.

BRIDGET It must be so inconvenient having had the muscles in your arm cut by a maniac.

LULU What? (*screams*) He's killing me! Help! Help! AAAAGGGGGHHHHH! AAAAAAGGGGHHHHH!

REVEREND DAVIDSON It's all right, Sadie Thompson. You're safe in God's house.

The Reverend calms Lulu. She comes back to the present.

BRIDGET I'm sure I didn't mean to upset her.

REVEREND DAVIDSON She's still recuperating. The love of God has not totally entered every pore of her body yet.

BRIDGET Well, that's certainly a shame. (*to Lulu*) I hope it happens soon.

They pause. They don't know what to talk about.

REVEREND DAVIDSON Mrs. McCrea, if you would continue the conversation please.

BRIDGET Yes. Certainly. Blah blah blah. I'm sorry. Where were we in the conversation? I've gotten a little lost.

REVEREND DAVIDSON We've discussed the weather. We said it was nice.

BRIDGET Yes, it's very nice. I really like good weather.

REVEREND DAVIDSON As a next step, why don't we begin by talking about the tea?

BRIDGET Yes, a good idea. Tea! How lovely. There's nothing so soothing as a nice cup of tea. Shall I pour?

REVEREND DAVIDSON Please.

BRIDGET Miss Thompson, will you have tea?

LULU I can't lift my arms.

BRIDGET So does that mean yes or no for tea?

REVEREND DAVIDSON Give her some tea. I'll lift the cup up to her lips and let her gently sip from my hand.

BRIDGET From your hand?

REVEREND DAVIDSON From the cup in my hand.

BRIDGET Maybe *I* should give her the tea. (*gives everyone tea during the following*)

REVEREND DAVIDSON Do what you want, it makes no difference to me.

BRIDGET Sugar?

REVEREND DAVIDSON No. Sugar is sweet and makes the body too active. I like my tea plain, or sometimes with milk.

BRIDGET Fine . . . three teas, no sugar, with milk.

LULU I don't like milk in my tea.

BRIDGET As time goes by, you will learn to like it.

REVEREND DAVIDSON All right, that's the tea discussion. I hope you noted it well, Sadie Thompson. Mrs. McCrea is a master of conversation, and you would do well to emulate her.

BRIDGET Oh, thank you, Reverend.

REVEREND DAVIDSON Now let's move on to a conversational topic not related to tea. Any suggestions?

BRIDGET I might tell you some things that my children did today.

REVEREND DAVIDSON That would be good if the room were filled only with women. But men cannot be expected to be interested in children, unless they're pedophiles. And then, of course, they should be castrated, put on a stick, and roasted over a pit. So don't tell us about your children.

BRIDGET Well, they're all grown anyway. The fifth one was just arrested for shoplifting.

REVEREND DAVIDSON Now that's a good topic.

BRIDGET Shoplifting?

REVEREND DAVIDSON No. What is wrong with the youth of our country nowadays.

BRIDGET It's all these liberal parents who don't discipline their children properly.

REVEREND DAVIDSON Did you neglect to discipline your children, Mrs. McCrea?

BRIDGET No, I should say I did not. I hit them, I cajoled them, I publically humiliated them, and two of them turned out beautifully. They cower when I enter a room, they never speak unless spoken to, and they are beautifully obedient. If you instructed them to slaughter the Jews, they would do it without a second thought.

REVEREND DAVIDSON We must hope they never hold the Nuremberg trials again.

LULU I'm sorry—something about slaughtering the Jews.

BRIDGET No, I said it wrong. I was making a point about how obedient my children were. The point was about obedience. That's how children learn right from wrong, by obeying and not questioning what's right and wrong, but just by *doing* it. And that's how two of these children of mine are. They're my joy. I tell them something and they agree. I, without thinking of it, said that they would kill the Jews if I asked them to, but, you see, I never would ask them to do that.

LULU But they would if you did? Obedience is so important to them?

BRIDGET Well, maybe they'd do it. You're missing the point. I was trying to point out the dangers of people thinking too much for themselves. The Nazis were wrong about the Jews. Let me make that very clear. One of my friends is Harriet Levin, and she is a lovely Jewish woman; I enjoy having lunch with her, and she is in favor of prayer in the public school, and she doesn't even mind if we put a Christmas crèche in the center of town on tax-supported grounds. So she's a lovely Jewish woman. So I don't know what the Nazis were talking about. No, if I told my children to exterminate anyone, it would be black people who don't work, black women who have too many children, homosexuals who flaunt their lifestyles in my face, and who misled my one son, who died, they killed him; and some closeted homosexuals as well. And, let me see, who else would I exterminate?

REVEREND DAVIDSON Unrepentant prostitutes?

BRIDGET Yes. If they are unrepentant, I would let my children exterminate them.

LULU Isn't killing against the law?

BRIDGET She wants to enter the conversation, and this is how she does it?

REVEREND DAVIDSON Sadie Thompson, Mrs. McCrea is a guest in my house, as are you. She is a woman of high moral caliber. It is wrong to challenge her and suggest that she wants to kill people. Nothing could be further from her mind.

LULU But I thought she just said she wanted to have her children kill people.

REVEREND DAVIDSON You were listening with an unsophisticated ear.

BRIDGET Of course, I don't want them to kill people. As I said, I was making a point about obedience. My two children—the ones who aren't the shoplifter—are very obedient young adults. They do everything I or my husband tell them to. They are a joy. And I have two other children who are all right, more or less, but not as good as the two who are totally obedient. They're sassy sometimes, I think it's the magazines they read. And I have one who killed himself—it was inevitable, drugs and sex, we told him they were wrong, I don't know why he didn't listen. It's the media. It's the schools. It's the availability of pornography, X-rated tapes. And now we have the one who's the shoplifter, we're praying for him a lot. And we pray for the dead one. (*cries*)

REVEREND DAVIDSON It would be appropriate to say something comforting to Mrs. McCrea.

LULU Uh . . . I'm sorry you're crying.

REVEREND DAVIDSON Offer hope somehow, Miss Thompson. Bring up God.

LULU God will . . . explain to you on the Last Day what went wrong with your children.

REVEREND DAVIDSON Well, that's all right, but sort of upsetting. Say God understands your pain and what a good person you are.

LULU God understands your pain. (*whispers*) Is she a good person?

BRIDGET (*suddenly harsh and pointed*) Well, you're the ex-prostitute, not me.

REVEREND DAVIDSON Ladies, ladies. This is not proper conversation. Time-out. Re-collect yourselves.

Pause

LULU The weather is very nice.

BRIDGET Yes it is.

LULU I'm glad you have the two children who turned out well. They must make you very proud.

REVEREND DAVIDSON Oh very good. That was an excellent conversational gambit.

LULU Thank you.

BRIDGET Yes, I am very proud of them. Jeffrey and Jennifer. My two J's. Everything they do pleases me and my husband. They live to please us, it's very gratifying. (*getting a bit argumentative*) So it was hypothetical when I said they would kill people when I asked them.

REVEREND DAVIDSON I wouldn't return to this subject, Mrs. McCrea.

BRIDGET No, but I'm just feeling judged here, like I'm a bad person, and I'm not a bad person. I'm a loving person. Very loving. And I was trying to analyze what it is about my two good children, and I realized their being obedient was a big part of it. "Honor thy parents," the Bible said.

LULU If a Jewish person heard you say your children were so obedient they'd kill the Jews if you told them to, they'd be very offended.

BRIDGET Look, I'm sorry I said it, but you're distorting what I said. Harriet Levin is my best friend, and she's Jewish, and when my son died, it was she who came over and sat with me and said she understood. Her son is married but he's very effeminate, and she's worried about it. He's also a hairdresser.

LULU Well, that must be very convenient for her. To get her hair done.

BRIDGET She wears a wig.

LULU Oh. Is she Orthodox?

BRIDGET Certainly not, she just has thinning hair. This conversation is going to hell. I think she's hopeless.

LULU I didn't bring up killing people.

BRIDGET Well, neither did I. And I would never tell my children to kill anyone unless it was clear to me that God wanted these people killed. Then I would try to do it through the law, but if gay people were molesting children or teaching so-called tolerance of a repugnant and death-causing lifestyle, well, then I would do what God required of me. And abortionists! I'd let them kill abortionists if God told me to. And, of course, it may come to that. I'm starting a list. (*takes out small pad, writing in it*)

LULU You say that God has told you to have an opinion. But how do you know you're hearing God's voice and not your own?

BRIDGET Well, that's a stupid question.

REVEREND DAVIDSON It isn't. It's a very good question. Congratulations, Sadie Thompson, you've asked a good question.

LULU Thank you.

BRIDGET Well, excuse me for living.

REVEREND DAVIDSON Here's how you know. You pray. You say, God, let me do thy bidding. God, give me a sign what I should do. You wait. Then when the sign comes, you follow God's bidding.

LULU But when I was having sex every 15 minutes, didn't I think that God was telling me to do this?

BRIDGET No, no, no. God never tells you to have sex. You were probably hearing the voice of the devil, isn't that so, Reverend?

REVEREND DAVIDSON Yes, Mrs. McCrea, it was the voice of the devil. Now, I think we should have a lighter topic of conversation. Let us discuss something humorous, or tell a joke. Mrs. McCrea, do you have a joke you could tell us?

BRIDGET Well, I'm in sort of a bad mood now. I can't just charge into telling a joke.

REVEREND DAVIDSON Yes, you two don't seem to have hit it off exactly.

BRIDGET Well, I don't like some recently repentant sinner to criticize the way I've lived my life.

LULU I'm sorry. I wasn't criticizing. I just reacted to the appalling thing you said about telling your children to kill Jews.

REVEREND DAVIDSON Ladies, ladies. Time-out. Silence for a moment. No more speaking.

All three are silent. The Reverend Davidson and Bridget sip tea.

BRIDGET I don't mean to complain, but this tea is tepid.

REVEREND DAVIDSON Very tepid. Now, what about my idea? Shall we graduate to the pleasantness of telling a joke? Who will start? Mrs. McCrea?

BRIDGET I'm not very good at jokes. Let me see. Do I remember any? Let me see. Ummm . . . Ummmm.

REVEREND DAVIDSON Well, if you don't . . .

BRIDGET No, I may, wait, I'm running through my memory . . . Let me see. Ummm . . . Ummmm.

REVEREND DAVIDSON If you don't have one, we needn't necessarily wait.

BRIDGET No, I think I have one. Let me keep trying to remember.

They all sit in silence for a bit. The Reverend Davidson seems a bit annoyed.

BRIDGET Yes. I have one! Are you ready?

REVEREND DAVIDSON Yes. I am very ready.

BRIDGET A duck walks into a drugstore and asks for a tube of lip balm. When asked to pay, the duck says: "Just put it on my bill."

The Reverend Davidson and Lulu stare at Bridget with no expression.

BRIDGET Well, I thought it was cute. My children liked it.

REVEREND DAVIDSON These are the obedient children, right?

Bridget looks annoyed and sips her tea. They all sip tea. The next topic doesn't come easily.

Cardinal O'Connor

Cardinal O'Conner was included in *Urban Blight,* an evening of sketches by twenty authors, which premiered May 18, 1988, at the Manhattan Theater Club in New York City.

Cardinal O'Connor	Rex Robbins

Subsequently, this sketch was part of *A Mess of Plays by Chris Durang* in 1996 at South Coast Repertory, in Costa Mesa, California, with Hal Landon Jr. as Cardinal O'Connor

VOICE And now, Cardinal John O'Connor will speak to you about the condom.

Enter CARDINAL O'CONNOR *dressed in red clerical robes; he is bouncing a basketball as he comes out, and is wearing sneakers.*

CARDINAL O'CONNOR Hi, there. I was just playing basketball with Mayor Ed Koch. Got a lot of baskets, didn't have time to change my sweatsocks. Hope I don't smell.

Anyway, I'm glad to be here today to talk to you about the condom.

Now it was reported in the *New York Times* that the National Bishops Committee, of which I am a member, just put out a statement about AIDS saying that even though contraception is objectively, morally wrong, that because not everyone else follows this Catholic belief, it might be acceptable to educate people that the condom can in some ways protect you from AIDS, as long as it was stressed that abstinence was the only 100 percent safe way, and as long as it was also stressed that contraception and condoms are wrong. So that's what the report said.

Well, this Bishops' report is not acceptable to me.

You can never justify a lesser evil by saying it prevents a larger evil. Now to put a condom on your penis is simply morally repugnant to God—as we in the Catholic Church have told you for centuries. And although Christ never talked about condoms, he made the Catholic Church His spokesman, and we have explained until we're blue in the face that sex is for procreation and that anything that interferes with procreation is wrong, it's wrong, it's wrong, it's wrong. Putting a condom on your penis is wrong.

I am a man of God, and I must point out to you what is wrong when it's wrong.

I don't care if it's not practical; I don't care if drug addicts and teenagers and homosexuals will run around giving each other AIDS and die—(*He stops abruptly. He realizes how this sounds and adds deep compassion to his voice.*) Well, that is, I do care, I care deeply about their suffering. (*His energy returns.*) But we can only tell them to use abstinence—to never have sex again for the rest of their lives.

That is the only morally acceptable advice I can give them.

I am unwilling to have any teenagers or drug addicts or promiscuous girls or homosexuals hear anything else.

I have never had sex in my entire life, and I'm healthy and normal, so I do not ask anyone to do anything that I myself would not be able to do, and have not done.

Let's start abstinence clubs around the country. It can be fun.

One other thing—people have said to me, you were an army chaplain, you supported the Vietnam War, you allowed men the lesser evil of killing one another to stop the greater evil of communism.

How can you be such a stickler and say that the lesser evil of condom use is somehow not balanced by its stopping the greater evil of spreading AIDS and causing great suffering and death?

And furthermore, Christ and the Bible say, "Thou shalt not kill," repeatedly throughout the Bible, and nowhere does anyone in the Bible say, "Do not put a little plastic balloon on your penis."

Well, I have a good answer to the people who say that. Here is my answer. My answer is about to follow. Here it comes.

Killing people for a good cause is not evil.

Putting a balloon on your penis, for whatever reason, is always, always evil.

I hope I have cleared up any misconceptions you may have had. And so, until the next moral crisis comes along and I need to tell you what's moral and what isn't, so long! (*Goes out cheerfully, bouncing his basketball.*)

The Book of Leviticus Show

The Book of Leviticus Show was filmed on video in the "public access" style for *Durang/Durang* at Manhattan Theater Club in New York City in 1994. It was included in the first preview, and then cut from the evening due to length. It had the following cast:

Lettie Lu	Becky Ann Baker
Tommy, her husband (off-camera)	Marcus Giamatti
Grandma	Patricia Elliott
Maggie Wilkinson	Lizbeth Mackay
Maggie's daughter	Keith Reddin
Two guests	David Aaron Baker, Patricia Randell

NOTE: The above cast list reflects the number of characters used in the video version filmed by director Walter Bobbie for the Manhattan Theater Club evening.

The script I have prepared is written so it can be done onstage rather than on video. (Doing it on video lets you capture the look of public access TV, but stage is probably easier.)

In the stage version, the characters of motel owner Maggie Wilkinson and her daughter do *not* appear.

CHARACTERS

LETTIE LU

TOMMY
her husband and cameraman

GRANDMA
Lettie Lu's mother

TWO GUESTS ON HER SHOW
a man and a woman

Optional Introduction

VOICE You are watching the Wheeling, West Virginia, Community Public Access Station, Channel 61. The West Virginia Community Public Access Station is in no way responsible for the content of any program on this channel. The views expressed belong to the public access individual producers. By law we must broadcast whatever people want to say. If we could shut down this entire public access station, we would be glad to. But by law we can't. So stay tuned for our next public access program, on Channel 61. We think it is a premiere episode.

Scene: A somewhat run-down motel room in West Virginia. A bed with an elderly GRANDMA *asleep on it. An empty birdcage. Suitcases around, opened, not quite unpacked. A standing screen, with clothes flung up over the top. A chair: Near the chair is* LETTIE LU, *about 35, in a print dress, wandering around. She has a fair amount of energy. Her husband* TOMMY *has a video camera, which he has trained on her. Tommy may best be out in the audience, or at the back of the theater.*

LETTIE LU Are we on the air?

Lettie Lu realizes that she is on the air; and talks out toward Tommy's camera. Sometimes she sits in her chair; sometimes she bounds up out of it, down to the edge of the stage, to be closer to the camera.

Hello there. Can you hear me? If you can't hear me, call 556-7421, and ask for Lettie Lu in Room 12, and then I'll talk up. This here is our first show, and so I don't know if I need to shout.

TOMMY (*from behind the camera*) You don't have to shout, Lettie.

LETTIE LU That's my husband Tommy. He's the cameraman. And this is Momma. Show Momma, Tommy. Momma is 83 years old and she brought me up all her life in West Virginia and she's a good woman. Bring the camera back to me, Tommy, people must be tired of looking at Momma. (*smiles at camera*) Hi again. I'm Lettie Lu and this is the first BOOK OF LEVITICUS SHOW installment. (*Lettie Lu holds up a cardboard sign with the hand-painted words, "BOOK OF LEVITICUS SHOW."*)

Now I was minding my business back in Tommy's and my house in West Virginia. The children had growed up, one of them is a country western star, one of them is a teller in a bank. Jimmy, he hasn't found himself yet, he don't do nothing. But we were havin' our quiet life when God set our house on fire. Well it wasn't God really, it was Momma; leastwise, we think it was Momma, she denies it, but who else was up cookin' at two in the morning, not me or Tommy, we wuz asleep.

But our house burned to the ground, all of it; and we wuz real bitter. We slept in the truck for a couple of nights, but then I said to Tommy, "What are we complainin' about, we got our lives. God gave us our lives, and we have got to be grateful."

And then we took the Bible out of the glove compartment, and I said, "Tommy, this is God's word, and it will comfort us." (*She picks up the Bible and shows us.*)

You know, you can open up the Bible to any old page and it will have a message for you. (*chooses a section at random*)

Like here, in the book of Numbers: (*she reads*)

"And the names of the men are these: of the tribes of Judah, Caleb the son of Jephunneh. And of the tribe of the children of Simeon, Shemeul, the son of Annihud. And the prince of the tribe of the children of Dan, Buddi the son of Jogli." Well this here don't mean a thing to us, but then we read that lovely passage about the Lord is thy shepherd and the green pastures, didn't we, Tommy?

TOMMY Yes, we sure did, Lettie.

LETTIE LU And we had some money in the bank, so we thought we'd just come on over to this motel, where the owner is a good Christian woman and her daughter with the harelip, but really it doesn't look bad if you don't look at it. And then Tommy said, "Lettie, read another passage from the Bible."

And then I turned to the book of Leviticus. (*reads with great importance*)

"And the man that committeth adultery with another man's wife, even he that committeth adultery with his neighbor's wife, the adulterer and the adulteress shall surely be put to death." (*bounces out of her chair to explain this*)

Well, that made a lot of sense to us because in all our years of marriage, and I married Tommy when I was fourteen or something, just like Loretta Lynn did, 'ceptin' I don't sing none; well, in all that time, Tommy and I has never been unfaithful to one another because we believe in God and religion and marriage. And I got to thinkin' about how people say they believe in the Bible but they don't follow through and do nothin' about it.

TOMMY Sit back down and read them the other part, Lettie.

Lettie Lu sits back down.

LETTIE LU Oh yeah. This is from the same page as the thing about adultery. (*reads from the Bible again*)

"And if a man also lie with mankind, as he lieth with a woman, both of them have committed an abomination, they shall surely be put to death." (*slams the Bible shut, bounces up again*) Well, we checked with the minister about the wordin' just to make sure we understood, but what we thought was true *was* true: this is about homos! And notice that God says *surely* someone will put them to death. I mean, God thinks it's so much what the right thing to do, that he just *presumes* somebody's gonna do it for him!

But we've gotten mighty far from followin' God's commands.

TOMMY Sit back down and get to the point, Lettie.

LETTIE LU You're right, Tommy. So what we done is, we went to Sally Bowden's house, and she's got herself two strappin' big sons, Big Jake and Big Harry, and we went into town and Big Jake and Big Harry went out and they captured an adulteress and a homo for us, and they tied 'em up and brung 'em here. I mean, they're here right now.

Lettie Lu goes and moves the screen. Behind it, tied up on the floor and with gags in their mouths, are a Woman and a Man. They struggle slightly; they've probably been there awhile.

See? I kept 'em behind the screen to add to the suspense. I hope you like our show. It's our first episode.

TOMMY Get back to the point, Lettie.

LETTIE LU Oh, right. And so now we're going to follow the teachings of God in the book of Leviticus. Wake up, Momma. (*Lettie Lu goes over to Grandma tries to wake her, but she seems to be sleeping deeply. To Grandma.*) We're gonna do the first ones. Momma. God, I hope she's not dead. Oh, there she goes. You havin' a dream, Momma?

GRANDMA Where's my teeth?

LETTIE LU Well, did you go to sleep with them in your mouth, or did you take them out first?

GRANDMA I don't know where they are.

LETTIE LU We know that, Momma. That wasn't the question. Now we are on television, and nobody out there wants to hear about your teeth.

GRANDMA I had a dream about pancakes.

LETTIE LU Pancakes? Oh dry up, Momma, you're irritatin' everybody. (*gets a gun from somewhere easy*) Old age is a terrible thing. Okay, you ready, Tommy?

Lettie Lu gets in a position, aims at the two people on the floor. Aims well, but maybe looks the other way; she's not blood-thirsty, just doing her best to follow the Bible.

Pay attention now, Momma, we're gonna kill 'em. In the name of God's will, you shall *surely* be put to death.

Lettie Lu fires the gun twice. One or both of the bodies twitch violently; because they're tied together, it's hard to tell if one or both have been hit.

Did I get 'em, Tommy?

TOMMY Looks like it. Wrap it up now, Lettie, we're outta time.

GRANDMA Do we know these people on the floor?

LETTIE LU (*annoyed to explain it again*) We met 'em in town, Momma, Jake and Harry tied 'em up, and I read in the Bible that God wanted somebody to kill 'em.

GRANDMA (*understanding*) Oh.

LETTIE LU Well, I'm gonna sign off now. Read your Bible, follow everything it says. And next week, we're gonna do the part from the book of Leviticus about how to sacrifice turtle doves to please God.

GRANDMA Where we gonna get a turtle dove?

LETTIE LU You're really awake now, aren't you, Momma? I don't know. Maybe Woolworths'll have one of those 98 cents parakeets and then I'll kill that.

GRANDMA Kill the parakeet?

LETTIE LU That's what it says in the Bible. God, you can't follow anything, it's amazing I grew up to be as smart as I am. Good-bye, all! God bless you! Tune in next week for more readings from *The Book of Leviticus Show*!

Lettie Lu waves at the camera. So does Grandma, though she looks back at the dead bodies a bit too. Music. Lights down.

Entertaining Mr. Helms

Entertaining Mr. Helms was originally written in 1990 for a "one minute play" benefit for the American Repertory Theater in Cambridge, Massachusetts (though it's more like six minutes).

Then it was performed again at a benefit for People for the American Way, in support of Harvey Gantt, who was running for the Senate against Mr. Helms. (Gantt lost, unfortunately, though he made a good showing.) At that benefit the rather star-studded cast for this sketch was:

Father	Stephen Collins
Mother	Sigourney Weaver
Son	Jace Alexander
Daughter	Danitra Vance

CHARACTERS

FATHER
Head of the household. Makes all the decisions. Knows best.

MOTHER
Friendly, lovely, charming. Defers to her husband. Does her best to be diplomatic if things are tense.

SON
Energetic, friendly, 16 years old. On the swim team.

DAUGHTER
Smart, though at age 14 she is still obedient to her parents.

NOTE: the Son and Daughter may be played by actors in their 20s if you like.

The sketch had the following introduction:

PERSON In 1989 Senator Jesse Helms of North Carolina pushed through legislation by which anyone who won a grant that year from the National Endowment for the Arts would have to sign a statement promising that they would produce no work that was obscene, including promises to refrain from (quote) "depictions of sadomasochism, homoeroticism, the sexual exploitation of children, or individuals engaged in sex acts" (unquote).

Although only a maniac would be in favor of sexual exploitation of children, following the other requirements would preclude works like Jean Genet's *The Balcony,* Michelangelo's statue of David, and the final chapter, at least, of James Joyce's *Ulysses.*

However, Mr. Helms undoubtedly knows best, and so this following piece was written at the time to try to please him. It is our hope to neither upset nor to offend anyone. Not any any any any any anyone.

The scene is the kitchen of an American home at breakfast time. Mother, father, two children of either sex. Sorry, scratch "either sex." Mother, father, daughter, son.

(If you wish to use the introduction, it can be done live by an actor, or done over the speaker system. Or if you wish to dispense with the introduction, perhaps you could explain the "Helms connection" in a program note. Or you can just do the sketch as it is, and let the title be slightly mysterious.)

A sunny, happy kitchen in a sunny, happy American home. FATHER, MOTHER, SON, DAUGHTER.

MOTHER Good morning, John. Good morning, Jane.

SON Good morning, Mother.

DAUGHTER Good morning, Mother.

SON AND DAUGHTER Good morning, Father.

FATHER Good morning. Hands on heart. (*Everyone places their hands on their hearts.*)

ALL OF THEM I pledge allegiance to the flag
Of the United States of America
And to the republic for which it stands
One nation, under God,
Indivisible, with liberty and justice for all.

FATHER Amen. Note if you will, it says "one nation, under God." It doesn't say under Satan, it doesn't say under agnostic. It says under *God*.

SON Yes, Father.

DAUGHTER Yes, Father.

MOTHER Now here's your delicious breakfast—breakfast is the most important meal of the day.

DAUGHTER Why doesn't Daddy ever make breakfast?

MOTHER Daddy makes the money to pay for the breakfast, and Mommy cooks it. That's how every single family in the United States is, and that's how the men and the women were in the Bible also. And please don't ask that question again.

DAUGHTER All right, Mommy.

FATHER What are you learning in your public schools that my tax money pays for, I'd like to know. John?

SON Well, in science class we're learning that it took God six days to make the world, and on the seventh day He rested. And we're learning that disease came about because Adam and Eve disobeyed God.

FATHER I'm happy to hear this. This science teacher sounds much better than your previous one, who I got fired.

MOTHER "Whom" I got fired, dear.

FATHER Oh, you're right. Thank you, darling. Children, listen to your mother when she speaks about grammar or cooking.

MOTHER The trick to making a three-minute egg is to cook it for 2 minutes and 45 seconds.

FATHER Ask me about arithmetic, however. And about morals. And about sports. John, how is gym class going?

SON Great, Dad. We played basketball yesterday, and one team was shirts, and the other team was skins, and I was on the skins team, and we . . .

MOTHER John, dear, don't talk about young men with their shirts off please, dear. We don't want to give the audience homoerotic ideas. Just say team A and team B.

SON Oh. Okay. Team A and team B; and then team B won.

FATHER Well, that's splendid.

SON Then we took our clothes off in the locker room, and we took showers.

MOTHER John!

SON Well, we were sweaty.

MOTHER John, go to your room.

SON What did I say?

FATHER John, you heard your mother.

SON All right. (*exits*)

MOTHER I hope there's nothing wrong with him. You know, Freud said there was a latency period.

FATHER Elizabeth, my God, don't talk about Freud. I'm sure John is fine. If he's not fine, we'll put him through aversion therapy. And if that doesn't work, we'll disown him.

DAUGHTER What are you two talking about? All he said was his team won at basketball.

MOTHER It was how he said it, darling. And don't call your parents "you two." Say "Mother and Father." Or "Mater and Pater."

DAUGHTER Yes, Mater and Pater.

FATHER Well, Jane, how is home economics going?

DAUGHTER Fine, except that Amy was hemorrhaging the other day.

MOTHER Really? Was it part of a class project?

DAUGHTER No, Mom, she had a homemade abortion because she was afraid to talk to her parents to get their permission for a regular one.

FATHER What's being said? I don't like this.

DAUGHTER Don't worry, Daddy, it'll never happen to me. Amy's a regular slut because she's such an emotional mess she keeps looking for love from boys and she doesn't know about contraception because you got our health teacher fired.

FATHER That woman was giving students a blueprint for prostitution.

DAUGHTER But that's just Amy, it won't happen to me. And you know why?

MOTHER Why, dear?

DAUGHTER Because I love you and Daddy, and I will always obey you, and I will never give the preciousness of my body to any boy until we're married and ready and capable of having a baby. I am a good girl, and I am pure. And I'm against abortion, and if only it was against the law, I would gladly turn my friend Amy in to the authorities, so she'd be put in jail if she wasn't already dead.

MOTHER Oh, we have raised a wonderful daughter.

FATHER We certainly have. I thank God for her. Thank you, Jesus.

MOTHER Jesus? Darling, I thought we were Jewish.

FATHER We were. But I've been thinking about Jesus a lot lately, and so many people I admire believe in him—Oliver North, John Poindexter, John Cardinal O'Connor. And I think it's time we converted. Enough of this chosen people business. The true chosen people are the Christians! Tomorrow morning after we say the Pledge of Allegiance, I want you all to have memorized the "Our Father."

MOTHER Oh. Well, this is a bit of a shift for me. And I think it will upset my parents. But you're my husband, and I love to obey you, and you know best in everything. (*Mother and Father kiss.*)

FATHER I certainly do. I don't understand why everyone doesn't agree with me all the time. I think all this disparity of opinion in our country is confusing to our children, and a great big waste of time. America works for me perfectly—I believe in God, I believe in prayer, I believe in military preparedness, I believe in heterosexuality, I believe in the authority of parents over their children, I believe in putting your toys away when you're done with them, I believe in knowing what's right, and doing what's right, and making sure everyone else knows and does what's right. To me, there is no room for difference of opinion when you're *right*. Am I right?

MOTHER You're right, darling. When you're right, you're right.

DAUGHTER You're right, Dad. You're far right! And I'm proud of you for it. Oh how I love my parents and my country. (*Enter son.*)

SON Dad, I'm sorry for what I said before. And I'm joining the Army. I want to be just like Oliver North.

MOTHER Oh, this is a happy day! We've become Christians, our daughter has told us she'll save her body until marriage, and now our son wants to join the military. To live in America is perfection! Who could ask for anything more? (*Mother and Father kiss. Son and Daughter smile and look on.*)

The Doctor Will See You Now

The Doctor Will See You Now was done onstage in New York City as part of a political revue produced by the Acting Company called *Issue? I Don't Even Know You.* The cast was as follows:

Woman Singer	Mary Lou Rosato
Mr. Nelson	Casey Biggs
Nurse Calliope	Kristine Nielson
Dr. Murgatroyd	Wayne Knight

CHARACTERS

WOMAN SINGER
happy and loud

MR. NELSON
the patient

NURSE CALLIOPE
the nurse

DR. MURGATROYD
the doctor

SCENE 1

A WOMAN SINGER *appears in a spotlight. She is dressed in a garish sequined dress with a flashy showbiz boa, as if she were a guest on some awful TV variety show. She sings a strident, upbeat song about the glories of love. She sings to the audience loudly, selling the song too hard, and energetically.*

After she sings a bit she says to audience:

WOMAN SINGER It's not just love that's sweeping the country.
Love isn't just from the neck up,
So best be safe, and get a checkup!

She sings the end tagline of the song. She smiles delightedly.

MAN'S VOICE The preceding has been a public service announcement.

Lights out on her.

SCENE 2

A doctor's waiting room, R.; and a doctor's office, L. The waiting room setting takes up less space; the doctor's office is bigger. At present only the waiting room part of the set is lit. In the waiting room is MR. WILSON, *a mild-looking man. And there is a* NURSE, *who is quite pretty and personable. Also sitting in the waiting room is the Woman Singer from a moment ago. She is still in her cabaret show glittering gown and boa, and so looks very odd in this setting. Mr. Wilson is reading a magazine. The Woman Singer is sitting, but staring ahead, attentive. The Nurse is on the phone.*

NURSE (*into phone*) I'll bring him in, doctor. (*gets up, crosses to Mr. Wilson*) The doctor will see you now, Mr. Wilson.

The Woman Singer bounds out of her seat and starts singing the same song she sang at the top of the piece. It is loud and sold very hard again.

Please, Mrs. Malloway, stop doing that. It's nerve-racking.

WOMAN SINGER (*petulant, insistent*) I want to see the doctor!

NURSE He's seen you already. There's nothing wrong with you. Physically. Besides, it's Mr. Wilson's appointment now.

WOMAN SINGER I'm not leaving here until the doctor gives me . . . medication! (*stamps her foot and smiles madly at the audience*)

NURSE I'll see what I can do.

Woman Singer sits back down. Nurse leads Mr. Wilson toward L., speaks to him.

(*To Wilson, friendly.*) She's really a nutcase, I'm afraid. The doctor has seen her twice already today, but she just won't go away.

MR. WILSON It must be difficult for you.

NURSE Yes. I never wanted to be a nurse. I wanted to be an encyclopedia salesman, but I couldn't carry the books. So I had to settle for this. Here's the doctor now.

Nurse brings Mr. Wilson into the office of DOCTOR MURGATROYUD; *L. R. should fade into darkness, with the Woman Singer seated back in her chair.*

I'll just leave you two here. (*exits*)

DOCTOR Fine woman. Reminds me of my mother. Hello, how are you feeling?

MR. WILSON Well, all right. It's just the pollen count is very heavy right now and, as I said last week, my allergies have been bothering me.

DOCTOR I see. Let me just look at your chart. (*looks at it*) Uh-huh. Uh-huh. Hmmmm. (*looks up at him*) I think I know what's bothering you.

MR. WILSON It isn't allergies?

DOCTOR No. It's VD.

Woman Singer bursts into the room, run after by the Nurse. Woman Singer sings her "Love" song at the top of her lungs, aiming it at the Doctor and Mr. Wilson and the audience.

NURSE I'm sorry, Doctor. She got away from me. Come along, Mrs. Malloway. (*Nurse drags out Woman Singer*)

DOCTOR That woman has strong lungs. No smoking there.

MR. WILSON I don't understand. I couldn't have VD. There's just me and my wife, and I haven't, and she hasn't . . .

DOCTOR Please give me a list of all recent contacts you've had. By state law we have to inform them that they may be infected. (*Hands him a form.*) There's room for eighty names and phone numbers. If you need more space, I'll give you another form.

MR. WILSON There haven't been any contacts. Do you have the right chart in front of you? I came to you last week for my allergies. I've been sneezing.

DOCTOR (*to intercom*) Nurse Calliope, would you come in here please? (*to Mr. Wilson*) Now, do you have a pen?

MR. WILSON I think there's been a mistake.

DOCTOR If you're unwilling to name names, by state law we are allowed to confiscate your address book and call everyone in it.

The Nurse enters during the above and goes behind Mr. Wilson's chair.

NURSE Is he ticklish?

She tickles him and at the same time removes his address book from his jacket pocket. Mr. Wilson squirms with the tickling.

MR. WILSON Stop that!

NURSE Here it is! (*takes his address book away*)

DOCTOR Now we'll start you on penicillin . . .

MR. WILSON But I'm allergic to penicillin.

DOCTOR Mr. Wilson, venereal disease is a national concern and a public disgrace. Please do not fight me on this.

NURSE How do you think he got it? (*doctor whispers to her*) Oh, bad Mr. Wilson. Shall I call his wife? (*looks at his chart, dials the phone*)

MR. WILSON I think you have my chart confused.

NURSE Well, let's see who answers the phone. I got the number from your chart. (*to phone*) Hello, Mrs. Wilson? (*to Mr. Wilson*) She said yes. (*to phone*) Mrs. Wilson, this is Nurse Calliope from Dr. Murgatroyd's office. By state law we have to inform you that you have been named as a possible contact by someone who has venereal disease. What? No, that's not the name. (*laughs; to Mr. Wilson*) She thought it was someone else. Who's Gregory? (*to phone*) No, Mrs. Wilson, it's your husband. Please make an appointment to see your physician as soon as possible. VD is a national problem. Did you know that there are 200 teenage pregnancies every five minutes?

During the above the Doctor has been taking Mr. Wilson's blood pressure, taking his temperature, otherwise keeping him involved. Mr. Wilson finally pulls away and goes to the Nurse.

MR. WILSON Give me the phone please. (*He reaches for the phone; Nurse slaps his hand.*)

NURSE Grabby. That's the kind of behavior that got you in this mess. (*to phone*) That's right. Every five minutes. (*hangs up*)

DOCTOR Are your parents still living?

MR. WILSON Yes, they are.

DOCTOR We have to call them. Nurse, find the number.

Nurse looks through book.

MR. WILSON This has gone far enough.

DOCTOR No, Mr. Wilson, it is you who have gone far enough. You went too far, and you must pay the consequences. Now, according to the government, I must by law inform the parents of anyone who wishes to purchase birth control or who has a venereal disease. (*to Nurse*) Have you found their number yet?

NURSE (*looking through book*) I'm still looking. Oooh, he knows Barry Manilow. I love him.

MR. WILSON It's a different Barry Manilow. Doctor, I know the president supported a law about telling parents of teenagers about if they ever wanted to get birth control, you know, a parental consent kind of law, I think, but it was never made into law, Congress didn't pass it . . .

NURSE (*looking at watch*) Ooops. There goes another teenage pregnancy.

MR. WILSON But even if they did pass it, I think you have the law confused. Surely the president doesn't mean for you to call up the parents of *adults*.

DOCTOR That is my understanding of the matter.

NURSE Oh, I found them. They're in a retirement village. (*starts to dial*)

MR. WILSON But you'll just upset them. And besides, I have an allergy, I don't have venereal disease.

DOCTOR Mr. Wilson, if you have lived a degraded life and have disgraced yourself by Lord knows what disgusting activities, at least be man enough not to deny it. Moral laxity is a national disgrace in our country, and the president and I, not to mention the House and Senate, *refuse* to put up with it. Isn't that so, Nurse Calliope?

NURSE Right. (*into phone*) Hello, is this Mrs. Wilson, the mother of Arthur Wilson?

MR. WILSON Give me that phone.

Doctor holds up a hypodermic.

DOCTOR You interfere with procedure, and by law I will be forced to inject you.

MR. WILSON What?

DOCTOR You heard me.

NURSE (*into phone*) Mrs. Wilson, I'm afraid I'm calling you about a family disgrace. Your son Arthur has that bad disease that begins with the letter "V."

MR. WILSON This is insane.

NURSE No, Mrs. Wilson, not venous thrombosis. (*laughs; to the room*) What a nut. (*to phone*) The first word rhymes with cereal.

MR. WILSON Mother, hang up. This is the beginning of fascism.

DOCTOR That's a rude and inflammatory remark. Now I'm going to have to inject you. (*Doctor jabs him with needle; Mr. Wilson falls over.*)

MR. WILSON (*fading, falling*) I . . . just . . . wanted . . . a simple antihistamine.

NURSE No, Mrs. Wilson, I don't mean Wheaties. It rhymes with the word "cereal," not with the brand name of a cereal. (*to Doctor*) I think she must be quite elderly. This may take a long time. (*to phone*) Starts with a "V." Uh-huh.

Nurse makes a face at the Doctor as if to say, "Isn't this fun?" The Doctor smiles back, and listens into the phone too, sharing the earpiece with the Nurse.

Yes, the second letter is a vowel . . . Uh-huh. Uh-huh.

The lights fade on the Nurse and the Doctor on the phone, but not to black. The Woman Singer enters and stands in front of the scene in a bright spot. She sings some more of her "Love" song again, then addresses the audience.

WOMAN SINGER La da da da, la da da da da . . . (*Spoken.*) It's sweeping the country. But don't sweep it under the carpet. We care about you. And so does your government. But remember, freedom has its limits. No one has the right to yell "fire" in a crowded theater, and no one has the right to play "Bolero" in the privacy of his or her own bedroom either. We can't let you make your own decisions. You're not smart enough. But don't worry. We're smart, and we'll do it for you! (*She smiles delightedly, and sings the final line of the "Love" song she had been singing.*)

MAN'S VOICE The preceding has been a public service announcement.

Under Duress: Words on Fire

Under Duress was part of *Words on Fire,* a program of pieces on fire or heat. It aired on PBS on *Alive from Off Center* in late 1990. It was produced by Wendall Harrington and directed by John Sanborn. The cast was as follows:

Chris	Christopher Durang
Stephanie	Kristine Nielson
Photographer	Peter Cunningham
Boy Scout	Charles Steinmann

CHARACTERS

CHRIS
a worried playwright

STEPHANIE
his trendy friend

PHOTOGRAPHER
who happens to be nearby

BOY SCOUT
(in slide)

Scene

A comfortable living room, morning. CHRIS, *a 30-ish author, addresses the audience.*

Sitting on a couch behind him, waiting for the scene to begin, is STEPHANIE, *an intense woman. She is dressed somewhat trendily.*

CHRIS Hello. How are you? I was remembering those four years we had with President George Bush, and a conversation I had with my friend Stephanie. So let's go back to that time. (*Chris crosses to his couch and sits down to speak with Stephanie.*) Hello, Stephanie.

STEPHANIE Hello, Chris. How's your writing going?

CHRIS Oh, you know.

STEPHANIE Yes. An artist's life.

CHRIS (*uncomfortable with talk of art*) Yes. Um . . . (*changes topic*) You know, I was reading this editorial in the paper about global warming, and how President Bush isn't doing anything about it even though all of his advisers, except one, have said he should do something right away, you know, about the emissions that cause global warming. But he's not doing anything. And then I had this dream about being really, really hot on the earth, and not being able to breathe. And things kept catching on fire. Do you think I should write him a letter? Or is it all pointless?

STEPHANIE I was reading *The Psychoanalysis of Fire* by Gaston Bachelard the other day.

CHRIS Oh yes?

STEPHANIE And I wrote down this quote to tell you, I thought it was so true. If I can just find it in my purse. (*goes through purse*)

CHRIS I've never heard of this book. Is it famous?

STEPHANIE Well, it's not on the best-seller list. Ah, here it is. Listen to this. "It is impossible to escape this dialectic: to be aware that one is burning is to grow cold; to feel an intensity is to diminish it; it is necessary to be an intensity without realizing it. Such is the bitter law of man's activity." (*looks at him significantly*)

CHRIS I'm sorry, I just got up a little while ago. Can you say it again?

STEPHANIE Maybe I didn't read it right. Let me do it again, emphasizing different words. (*stressing words oddly*) "It is *impossible* to escape this *dialectic:* to be aware that one is *burning* is to grow *cold;* to *feel* an *intensity* is to *diminish* it; it is necessary to *be an intensity* without realizing it. *Without realizing it.* Such is the bitter law of man's activity. Such is the *bitter* law . . . (*makes "bitter taste" faces*) . . . of man's activity."

CHRIS I don't know if I really followed it.

STEPHANIE Maybe I should do it again.

CHRIS No, please, don't. Let me look at it. I can't hear it aloud, I don't think. (*looks at it*) What is "dialectic" again? Two opposing thoughts or something?

STEPHANIE Didn't you read Marx? He used the word "dialectic" constantly.

CHRIS I didn't read Marx. I went to Catholic school.

STEPHANIE Oh. Well, "dialectic" means . . . "ideas, thoughts . . ." "coming to ideas by logic." I think. Let's move past that word.

CHRIS Uh-huh. "To be aware one is burning is to grow cold." All right, he's not talking about actually being burned, like with boiling water, right? I've been burned, it isn't to grow cold.

STEPHANIE No, I don't think Gaston means actually being burned. I think he means to be burning in an intellectual sense—like having a "fever of ideas."

CHRIS (*trying to make sense*) All right, a fever of ideas. When you are in a fever of ideas and you are aware of it, you grow cold—and the fever of ideas dwindles down to a . . . trickle of cool, non-feverish ideas.

STEPHANIE Well, less elegantly, but yes.

CHRIS (*reads again*) "To feel an intensity is to diminish it; it is necessary to be an intensity without realizing it." So when you're fired up with an idea, or feeling, and you start to be conscious about it, the passion you feel diminishes because of this consciousness, and so . . . (*cranky, frustrated*) And so *what*? This thought is so abstract, it makes me want to scream.

STEPHANIE Well, you're reading it out of context.

CHRIS Is the whole book this way?

STEPHANIE If I had known you were an anti-intellectual, I wouldn't have taken the quote out of my purse.

They sit in silence for a moment.

CHRIS So, do you think I should write George Bush?

STEPHANIE What about?

CHRIS This global warming thing.

STEPHANIE I really couldn't say.

CHRIS Well, don't be mad about the quote, Stephanie.

STEPHANIE I will be mad about it. I make perfectly good conversation, then *you* do an endless dialectic, and you make me feel . . . stupid.

CHRIS You're not stupid. I just couldn't follow the quote.

STEPHANIE Yes, you made that evident.

CHRIS Let's talk about something else.

STEPHANIE What, global warming? Your topic?

CHRIS It's not my topic. But it's really serious. I mean, if the scientists are right and temperatures go up and stay up, then the polar caps will melt and the sea levels will rise, and there'll be famine and disease and death for our children.

STEPHANIE We don't have children.

CHRIS Well, for other people's children.

STEPHANIE Well, I have to go now.

CHRIS Oh, all right. Thanks for coming by.

STEPHANIE You're welcome. Will I see you at Pamela's opening?

CHRIS Who's Pamela?

STEPHANIE I guess I won't. Good-bye.

CHRIS I'll see you to the door. (*Chris walks her to the door of his apartment, opens the door.*) Good-bye.

STEPHANIE Good-bye.

She exits. Chris looks back to the audience.

CHRIS (*to audience*) I guess I upset Stephanie. I didn't mean to. Maybe if I read the quote in another mood, I would've liked it. I found it hard to understand. Excuse me, I'm going to try to write this letter to the president.

Lights dim. The sound of typing. On a screen we see projected a few slides of Chris typing a letter at his computer: He looks intense, focused. The sound of typing stops. Lights back up on Chris, holding his finished letter, sealed in an envelope. He waves the letter in his hand.

(*to audience*) Well, I finished it. (*looks at it, thoughtfully*)

Now the problem with the letter is that it's in sentences. And judging from the presidential campaign, maybe George Bush only understands sound bytes. (*thinks*)

I don't know that he'll follow it. Maybe I better redo this letter in sound bytes, and with photo opportunities. I better find a photographer.

Lights change. On the screen we see a slide of Chris shaking hands with a photographer, then of posing in front of a photographer's white backdrop. Then we see a series of slides of Chris in poses, while the real Chris stands nearby reciting his sound bytes. First pose in slide: Chris dressed in suit, looking respectable, but holding his collar out, as if it's hot.

(*live*) Hey, George! Earth hot!

Moves his collar back and forth, fans his face, makes uncomfortable faces. Second pose in slide: Chris stands by 9-year-old BOY SCOUT. *Chris has hand on Boy Scout's head, paternal.*

(*live*) George: strong leader needed!

Third pose in slide: Chris dressed as fireman, with heavy fireman coat and helmet.

(*live*) Don't risk future inferno!

Fourth pose in slide: Chris, back in suit, in front of many, many candles, either on a table or on a birthday cake.

(*live, with urgency*) Thousand points of light, heating up! Fire fire fire!

Fifth pose in slide: Chris, still in suit, but wearing a Carmen Miranda fruit hat and earrings for some reason.

(*live*) Don't wait, act now.

Sixth pose in slide: Chris, just in suit again, holding Monopoly play money in one hand and a plastic balloon globe of the world in the other.

(*live*) Which more important—money or continuation of planet?

Seventh pose in slide: Chris seated on ground next to a sweet-looking dalmatian. The dalmatian looks placid and has a letter in his mouth.

(*live*) Dear George. Letter to follow.

The slide show is finished. Lights offscreen. Lights focus back more clearly on Chris in living room.

(*to audience*) Wow. That was exhausting. And I think the photographer's bill will be large. And who knows if Bush will understand what I've said; you can't really make an argument in sound bytes. I should really just send the original letter I wrote, and forget about the sound bytes. (*looks down at the envelope*)

Oh. But I need to buy a stamp. Ohhhhhh. (*spirals down into depression*)

Uhhhhhhh, and the lines in the post office are so long. It'll take hours. And sometimes the postal employees go crazy and shoot people, and he probably will never read the letter anyway, and what can just one person do, it all seems so hopeless. Maybe I should just forget the letter. Maybe I'll be *dead* before the global warming thing gets bad enough. (*deflates to nothing almost; then looks out at audience*)

But that's no way to behave, is it? The individual does count, doesn't he? And even if he doesn't entirely, we have to act as if we do, don't we? I think so. Right. Right. (*recaptures his energy and intention*)

Okay, okay! I'm ready. I will go to the post office. I will buy the stamp. I will send the letter. Here I go. Good-bye!

Chris waves good-bye to audience and leaves through his apartment door. The door shuts with purpose behind him.

An Altar Boy Talks to God

(*Adapted from a section of* LAUGHING WILD)

An Alter Boy Talks to God was first produced as part of *A Mess of Plays by Chris Durang* at South Coast Repertory, in Costa Mesa, California. The evening was directed by David Chambers, and the cast for this piece was as follows:

Robert	Robert Patrick Benedict
God	Hal Landon Jr.

CHARACTERS

ROBERT
a young man

GOD
God

Scene

ROBERT, *a young man, comes out and stands in a spotlight. He talks directly to the audience. He is friendly and outgoing with them.*

ROBERT I used to be an altar boy; from about age 8 to age 14. I used to ring the little bell when the priest would hold up the Eucharist. And I used to swing the little iron pot thing that was filled with incense when it was Lent. And I used to hand the priest things . . . like a holy napkin to wipe his mouth after he drank the wine that wasn't just wine but was Christ's blood transubstantiated.

I'm sort of sorry I wasn't an altar boy back when it was all in Latin. I have an older brother who's like 20 years older than me . . . 'cause I'm the youngest of 8 children, and so the age spread in our family is really big; I have a couple of nephews who are older than me . . . do you follow that?

Anyway, this older brother of mine said it was a lot more exciting to be an altar boy back when it was in Latin. The priest would say "Kyrie Eleison," and then you'd say back, "Et cum spiritu tuo." And now instead the priest says, "The Lord be with you," and then the whole congregation, not just the altar boy, says, "And also with you."

But, like, nobody in their right mind says, "And also with you." It sounds like you're talking from a foreign-language dictionary. I mean, you might say, "And you too." Or "Thanks, buddy, same to you." But you don't say, "And also with you."

So anyway, I missed the whole church in Latin thing, but it sounded interesting.

And then I stopped being an altar boy at about age 14 because I was on the swim team and I practiced so much I didn't want to have to get up for 8 A.M. Mass on Sunday. So I went to twelve noon Mass with my parents and with some of my nephews, who are older than me.

And then one of these nephews got AIDS. It was very hush-hush. It was early in the epidemic, and people didn't know much about it except it was really awful and that if you got it through a blood transfusion or because you were a hemophiliac, well, then, that wasn't so bad, I mean, nothing to be ashamed of. But if you got it from using a hypodermic to shoot drugs or because of some sexual act you shouldn't be doing, well, then, this was considered embarrassing, and you and your parents should only talk in a whisper.

And then some fundamentalist-type people started to say that God had sent AIDS as a punishment to gay people. And I thought to myself, wow . . . this doesn't fit my idea of God. So I went to heaven, and I asked God what it all meant.

The stage changes. A curtain opens, or lights shift, and we see GOD *seated in a lounge chair, drinking an iced tea or something. God is an older man, a bit cranky, wearing a loose robe. Robert goes up to God.*

Hello, God.

GOD Hello. Who are you?

ROBERT I used to be an altar boy.

GOD Oh yes, hello.

ROBERT What can you tell me about AIDS and gay people?

GOD Boy, oh boy, do I hate homosexuals. And so I've given them a really horrifying disease.

ROBERT (*surprised*) Really?

GOD Yes. And drug addicts . . . and hemophiliacs.

ROBERT But why hemophiliacs?

GOD Oh, no reason. I want the disease to go through the bloodstream, and I can't figure out how to send the disease through the bloodstream and not affect hemophiliacs.

ROBERT Yes, but aren't you all powerful? Can't you make the disease just hit the people you want it to hit?

GOD Well, you'd think I could, but I can't seem to. And so if hemophiliacs get it, well . . . the suffering will be good for them.

ROBERT Really? In what way?

GOD Oh, I don't know. I'll explain it at the end of the world.

ROBERT I see. Tell me, what about the children of drug addicts? Will they get the disease through their mother's wombs?

GOD (*suddenly realizing this*) Well—why not? Serve the hophead mothers right. Boy, oh boy, do I hate women drug addicts!

ROBERT Yes, but why punish their babies?

GOD And I hate homosexuals!

ROBERT Yes, yes, we got you hate homosexuals . . .

GOD Except for Noël Coward, he was droll.

ROBERT Yes, he was droll.

GOD And I hate Haitians! Anything beginning with the letter "h."

ROBERT Goodness. But isn't it unfair to infect innocent babies in the womb with this dreadful disease?

GOD Look, homosexuals and drug addicts are very, very bad people; and if babies get it, well, don't forget I'm God, so you better just presume I have some secret reason why it's good they get it too.

ROBERT Yes, but what is this secret reason?

GOD Stop asking so many questions . . .

ROBERT Yes, but . . .

GOD There you go again, trying to horn in on the Tree of Knowledge just like Adam and Eve did. Boy, oh boy, does that make me wrathful!

Okay, you ask me questions and irritate me, I'm going to give AIDS to 3,000 more homosexuals. Pow! How do you like that?

And 7,000 more drug addicts. Pow! And to little Mary Johnson in Hoboken, New Jersey, she's a hemophiliac, pow! And to a whole bunch of Haitians . . . pow! pow!

Oh . . . and I hereby revoke penicillin. Anyone out there who has ever been exposed to syphilis will suffer and die just like they used to—as a side issue, I love to connect sex and death, I don't know why I invented sex to begin with, it's a revolting idea, but as long as I have, I want it done *properly* in the missionary position with *one* person for life, or I want those who disobey me to die a horrible death from AIDS and syphilis and God knows what else. Is that clear?

ROBERT Very clear. Well, good-bye.

Robert walks to another area of light; lights dim on the area God is in.

Well, I don't think that was really God, do you? I think that was a rageaholic somewhere. Or a projected image of some really angry people. But it wasn't God, and it wasn't heaven. I think it's harder to get to heaven and talk to God than I thought.

The Hardy Boys and the Mystery of Where Babies Come From

The Hardy Boys and the Mystery of Where Babies Come From was first produced by New Mercury Group at Dixon Place, in New York City, on February 24–26, 1997, with three plays written by Craig Lucas, Perry Laylon Ojeda, and Lanford Wilson. The evening was produced and directed by Randy Gener; the lighting and sound designs were by Yossi Wanono; the costume design was by Moira L. Shaughnessy; the projection design was by Joe E. Jeffreys and Randy Gener; the prop manager was Ellen Esposito; and the production stage manager was Bob Speck. The cast was as follows:

TV Announcer's Voice	Jordan Schildcraut
Frank Hardy	John-Michael Lander
Joe Hardy	Sam Trammell
Nurse Ratched	Mike Jefferson
Mr. Hardy	Michael Edward O'Connor

This production was remounted at LaMama, Etc., with the same cast, except for Sam Trammell, who was unavailable and who was replaced by Matthew Vipond.

The Hardy Boys was also done as part of *Mix and Match Durang* at the John Drew Theater in East Hampton, New York, in 1997, directed by Elizabeth Gottlieb, with Jonathan Walker as Frank Hardy, Michael Ian Black as Joe Hardy, Jennifer Van Dyck as Nurse Ratched, and Peter Jacobson as Mr. Hardy.

CHARACTERS

FRANK HARDY
a cute young man

JOE HARDY
another cute young man

NURSE RATCHED
a terrifying nurse

MR. HARDY
Frank and Joe's father

SCENE I

Scene: The Hardy Boys' bedroom. Bunk beds. Posters on the wall.

If possible, a screen upstage that has titles from time to time. (This can also be done with a voice over the speaker system if you prefer.) At the top of play on the screen we see the title: THE HARDY BOYS AND THE MYSTERY OF WHERE BABIES COME FROM.

Music plays underneath the title (somewhat ominous mystery music, mixed with weekly dramatic TV series music).

FRANK HARDY *sits at his desk. He is around age 20, nice-looking, preppy, wearing a collegiate sweater.*

JOE HARDY, *his brother, comes in. He's around age 20, nice-looking, preppy, wearing a collegiate sweater.*

JOE Hi, Frank.

FRANK Hi, Joe.

JOE Neat sweater, Frank.

FRANK Yours too, Joe.

JOE Dad gave me mine.

FRANK He gave me mine too.

JOE Dad's great.

FRANK Yeah, he is. Great.

JOE You wanna play Monopoly?

FRANK Not now.

JOE Chess?

FRANK No, you have to think too hard.

JOE Clue?

FRANK No, but you're getting closer. Why don't we do some sleuthing?

JOE Oooh, I love the word "sleuthing," Frank. It makes me feel excited right in the pit of my stomach.

FRANK Me too. It's a great word.

JOE Is there some mystery to solve, Frank, that we can use our sleuthing powers on?

FRANK Yes, Joe, there is. But let's change sweaters first.

Lights change, dimmer. Music. We watch Frank and Joe put on different sweaters. Then on the screen [or on the loudspeaker] A FEW MINUTES LATER. Lights come back up, full, on the bedroom. The boys regard their different sweaters.

JOE Nice sweater, Frank.

FRANK Yours too, Joe.

JOE Now what's the mystery?

FRANK Well, I heard someone at school say that Nancy Drew may have to get married because "she has a bun in the oven."

They both look baffled.

JOE Gosh, Frank, that doesn't make any sense at all. Our housekeeper Mrs. Danvers has had whole cakes in the oven, and she's never had to get married.

FRANK That's just it. Something's fishy here.

JOE (*shudders pleasurably*) I love the word "fishy." It makes me feel excited right in the pit of my stomach.

FRANK Me too, Joe. And you're right—this whole thing *doesn't* make sense. Let me think. (*thinks*) No, it hurts.

JOE Well how shall we solve this mystery? I know—let me interrogate you! Frank, who told you this crazy thing about "buns in the oven"?

FRANK I don't remember.

JOE Well, that finishes that investigation.

FRANK No—wait. The school nurse said it!

JOE Nurse Ratched! (*sound of ominous music*) Gosh, that music sure is ominous. I wish Mrs. Danvers would leave our stereo system alone. Maybe we can get Dad to fire her. Then it would be just guys living in the house. I'd prefer that.

The ominous music fades out.

FRANK Me too. At least she doesn't sleep here.

JOE And she's so crazy. Always trying to get me to jump out the window.

FRANK That's just her sense of humor.

JOE Well, I don't find it funny. Women are terrifying, aren't they?

FRANK That's what Dad always said.

JOE Say, speaking of terrifying women, maybe we should go see Nurse Ratched and ask her what she meant about all this bun-in-the-oven stuff.

FRANK We *could* ask her, but that seems too simple.

JOE Why don't we do some *sleuthing* then? (*shudders with delight*) Oooooh, my stomach again. It's just like late at night when I . . . well, never mind. Why don't we go see Nurse Ratched, but we won't actually ask her anything, we'll pretend we're sick, and we'll kinda talk around things listening for clues, and that way it'll still be *sleuthing*! Ooooooh!

FRANK That's a good idea, Joe. But let's change sweaters first.

JOE Okay.

As the lights fade and series music plays, the boys start to take off their sweaters. On the screen we see: END OF EPISODE ONE.

SCENE 2

The stage changes (or lights shift) to the School Nurse's office.

NURSE RATCHED *is there, looking through the men's underwear section of the Sears, Roebuck catalog.*

On the screen we see: EPISODE TWO.

Frank and Joe come in, wearing new sweaters.

FRANK Hello, Nurse Ratched.

NURSE RATCHED Well, hello, boys. Nice sweaters. What can I do you for?

JOE We wanted to ask you a que . . . (*Frank jabs him in the ribs.*)

FRANK One of us is sick. We think it might be strep throat.

NURSE RATCHED Strep throat, huh? Which one of you has it?

JOE We're not sure. We thought you better examine both of us.

NURSE RATCHED Sure, I'll examine you. Oh, you boys are so cute, I could eat you up!

FRANK Eat us up . . . like "buns in the oven"?

NURSE RATCHED No, not like buns in the oven. Like hot dogs! *(laughs hysterically)*

JOE Gee, another terrifying woman whose sense of humor I don't understand.

NURSE RATCHED Now which of you is Frank, and which of you is Joe, I get confused.

FRANK I'm Frank.

JOE And I'm Joe.

NURSE RATCHED And I'm ready for action. (*laughs hysterically*) Oh, I'm going to be fired if I don't watch it. I just love young men. That's why I took this job. All right, boys, take your shirts and pants off, I want to look at your throats.

JOE Okay, but you gotta promise that you'll talk some more about buns in the oven.

NURSE RATCHED Sure. Hot cross buns, French pastries, French movies, X-rated X-rays. Anything you want, Joe.

JOE Frank.

NURSE RATCHED I thought you said you were Joe.

JOE Oh, I'm sorry, I am Joe. I just got confused.

FRANK You bozo.

NURSE RATCHED Okay, boys, now take off your clothes.

Ominous music. The boys start to remove their sweaters. Lights out on them. On the screen we see a picture of a large clock, which is at three o'clock. This picture of the clock fades into the same clock, later, at 7:15. Lights come back on the Nurse's office. The lighting suggests twilight a bit, maybe has some orange coming in from the side. Frank and Joe are in T-shirts and boxer shorts, tied up back-to-back on the examining table. They are alone.

FRANK I didn't know they had to tie you up to check for strep throat.

JOE Neither did I.

FRANK Okay, let's add up the facts we know so far about the mystery.

JOE Well, Nurse Ratched says we don't have hernias because she gave us that coughing test for two hours.

FRANK All right, that's fact number one. What else?

JOE Well, she thinks we're cute.

FRANK I think we're cute too, but we need more clues than that to solve this mystery. Nancy may be in trouble!

JOE I find it hard to think all bundled up this way. I wonder when Nurse Ratched is coming back with the bicycle pump?

MR. HARDY, *Frank and Joe's father, comes into the Nurse's office, wearing a suit and looking annoyed.*

MR. HARDY Frank, Joe! What are you two boys doing here all tied up?

FRANK We're sleuthing, Dad.

JOE Ooooo-ooooooh.

MR. HARDY You two boys really are retarded. I should have my sperm analyzed. Don't you know that Nurse Ratched is a sex maniac?

JOE Gosh, Dad, no! Is she?

FRANK Wow. And what's sperm?

JOE And what's sex, and what's maniac, and what's retarded?

FRANK And why should Nancy have to get married because of some breakfast food she has in her oven?

MR. HARDY What? Breakfast food?

FRANK There must be some reason she has to get married.

MR. HARDY She's pregnant.

Joe and Frank look at each other, astonished.

FRANK Pregnant!

JOE Gosh!

FRANK What's pregnant?

MR. HARDY Well, I guess you boys are old enough to be told the facts now. I kinda wanted to wait until you were 35 or so, but maybe now that you already know this much, I better tell you the rest. Okay, fellas, listen up. I'm about to explain where babies come from.

JOE Babies! What do babies have to do with buns in the oven?

MR. HARDY Well, it's complicated, and a little bit disgusting.

FRANK Go ahead, Dad, we can take it.

MR. HARDY We'll start with the flower and the bee. The bee pollinates the flower, by taking pollen from the stamen and delivering it to the pistil, which in the human species is like fertilizing the egg, which is . . .

Nurse Ratched appears behind Mr. Hardy and puts a cloth soaked in chloroform over his mouth.

NURSE RATCHED That's about all the filth I think the boys should learn today, Mr. Hardy.

Mr. Hardy falls to the floor.

JOE Gosh, Dad, you've been chloroformed. (*to Nurse Ratched*) Why did you do that? Are you crazy?

NURSE RATCHED Is the pope Catholic?

JOE I don't know. He's Polish. Is he Catholic too?

FRANK Wait, Joe, we got some clues from Dad right before he lost consciousness. He said something about eggs, and you make eggs on *top* of the oven, while you make buns *inside* of the oven. Maybe there's some clue about being on top, and being inside.

JOE It doesn't ring any bells with me, Frank. I think we have a lot more *sleuthing* to do, ooooo-oooooh.

NURSE RATCHED Something make you shiver, honey?

FRANK The bee, the flower. Inside, on top.

NURSE RATCHED That's very nice. That's almost a haiku.

JOE Hi coo? Gosh, I just don't understand women.

NURSE RATCHED That's 'cause we have different hormones.

JOE I heard about that in health class. We had to do a paper on what makes a hormone.

NURSE RATCHED And what makes a hormone?

JOE I don't know. I got an F. Is that a good grade?

NURSE RATCHED Oh, I like a good F.

FRANK Can you go away for a minute? I need to think.

NURSE RATCHED Well, I'll be right back, and then we'll take some pictures. (*She leaves.*)

FRANK I'm so confused. I feel we're on the brink of learning a really big mystery, but I'm finding it hard to concentrate because we're all tied up in our underwear, and that crazy woman keeps coming in here acting all funny.

JOE But she said she wasn't crazy. She said she was a Polish Catholic.

FRANK I don't know. (*sees something, tense*) Joe, look! (*Frank and Joe look over to a corner, where their sweaters lie in a heap.*) Joe. She didn't even fold our sweaters!

JOE Gosh.

FRANK Joe—I think maybe she *is* crazy.

Ominous music. On the screen we see: END OF EPISODE TWO. Then we see: NEXT WEEK FRANK AND JOE JOIN A HEALTH CLUB AND GET A FUNGUS IN A STRANGE PLACE. Music finishes.